# Questions you always wanted to ask about English

# Questions you always wanted to ask about English*

*but were afraid to raise your hand

by

Maxwell Nurnberg

GOYAL SaaB

GOYAL Publishers & Distributors (P) Ltd.

86, UB, (University Block) Jawahar Nagar, Delhi - 110007

Ph.: 23852986, 23858362, 9650597000 Fax: 23850961

E-mail: goyal@vsnl.com; Website: www.goyalsaab.com

www.goyalpublisher.com

**This Indian Edition 2005**
First Indian Edition 1998



This special low priced Indian Reprint is published by arrangement with the original American publisher, for sale in India and is the only authorised, complete and unabridged reprint of the latest original edition.

Published in india by Ashwani Goyal
for ***W.R. Goyal Publishers & Distributors***
86, U.B. Jawahar Nagar, Delhi - 110007
Tel.: 23852986, 23858362 Fax : 23850961
E-mail : goyal@vsnl.com

*To Rose and Ellen*

## Acknowledgments

For the many sentences adapted and adopted from the daily press, I am especially indebted to the writers—most of them anonymous—of AP, UPI, and *The New York Times.* I have also used an occasional sentence from the *Saturday Review* and *The New Yorker.*

Since I have used so much current material, I wish to make the usual disclaimer: The opinions expressed in these excerpts do not necessarily express my views or those of Washington Square Press.

For material other than newspaper excerpts I should like to make the following acknowledgments:

To Evelyn Hammett for her delightful "Mourning Becomes the Apostrophe," originally published in *Word Study,* a Merriam-Webster publication.

To Nona Balakian of *The New York Times Book Review* staff for excerpts from her brilliant article: "Topics: Style and the New Economy." Copyright, ©, 1965, by the New York Times Company.

To Gore Vidal for his comments on the colon and the comma, which appeared in and were part of the aforementioned article.

To Goodman Ace for the excerpt from his column "Top of My Head." Copyright, ©, 1971, by *Saturday Review.*

And, finally, to my wife, Rose, for her patient assistance and good advice.

## About the Author

Maxwell Nurnberg, Adjunct Professor of English, New York University, was Chairman of the English Department of Abraham Lincoln High School, Brooklyn, New York, for 35 years. He enjoys writing books on language in such a way as to make them fun for the reader. Among his other books are *What's the Good Word?* 1970). *Wonders in Words A Gathering of Poems* (Editor) *Fun with Words* and *Word Play* (1971).

He has co-authored with Dr. Morris Rosenblum *How To Build a Better Vocabulary* and *All about Words*

**Would you rather be right than hesitant?**

Learning to sharpen your tools of communication is fun with this unusual manual by Maxwell Nurnberg. His skillful approach, supported by a keen sense of humor, will inform as well as amuse the reader who needs a handy reference book to answer many troublesome questions.

# Contents

## A Word to the Reader

If you are reading this sentence, I feel safe in assuming that you are interested in improving your use of English and that you have questions you'd like to have answered about the language you speak and write. You may even want to know how the language has changed through the years, how sometimes "correctness" is not determined by the rigid rules of grammar but by the weight of usage and general practice.

While I most certainly agree that language is a living, growing thing, shaped and changed by usage, I demur when the usage that is accepted as standard by some is not that of the "best" writers or speakers. Would any of them ever say or write "momento" for "memento"? Yet *Webster's Third New International Unabridged Dictionary,* copyright 1961 (hereafter referred to as Webster III), not only gives "momento" in bold type as a variant of "memento" but has a separate entry for it! (It must be added in fairness that *Webster's Seventh New Collegiate Dictionary,* copyright 1971, based on Webster III, does not even mention "momento.") As one of the newer dictionaries—and one of the best, certainly—Webster III seems to be the most permissive.

By comparison with Webster III, *The American Heritage Dictionary of the English Language* (1969) seems conservative. One of the unusual features of this handsome dictionary is the poll it took of 104 experts (chosen from among "novelists, essayists, poets, journalists, writers on science and sports, public officials, professors"—all well known in their special fields) on questions of disputed usage (hereafter referred to as the Usage Panel). Their decisions, given in percentages, often lean in varying degrees toward the traditional.

As between loose and strict constructionists, I walk the eclectic middle of the road, sometimes stepping onto the shoulders. But being a guide, I now and then call attention to the views on the left side of the road and those on the right. Therefore, as you read on in this book, you may detect a certain inconsistency. For in describing the problems of usage and grammar I often indicate general practices that bypass the traditional rules, yet in the exercises that follow—just for practice—the "correct" grammatical forms are insisted upon.

This is done so that later on you can make the choices you are most comfortable with. When you do this you will at least *know* what the strictly grammatical form is—if only to rebel against it!

However, don't sell conventional grammar short or the power it still exerts on the American public. When an American soft-drink advertiser buys a whole page in color in *The New York Times Magazine* as well as spots on radio to tell you large and clear that his product AIN'T GOT NO SUGAR, he knows it will catch your attention—instantly. In an earlier campaign, another advertiser, knowing the effectiveness of using a disputed "like" in his copy, bombarded listeners with the persistent question, "What do you want? Good grammar or good taste?" (lavishly orchestrated, sung, and choreographed).

Well, if you read this book, maybe you can have both good taste and "good" grammar. And perhaps some fun as well.

# Questions you always wanted to ask about English

Chapter 1

# Does It Make Any Difference to You?

"I don't need none," shouted the lady of the house even before the young man at the door had had a chance to say anything.

"How do you know, lady?" he said. "I just might be selling grammar books."

Do you find yourself wondering whether to use *imply* or *infer*, look uneasy as you blurt out *for my brother and I*, or fear the silence that may follow when you say, "I am a student here now for two years"? Do you break into a cold sweat when faced with a choice between *who* and *whom*, go tongue-tied in the presence of *was* and *were*, or hesitate when confronted by *good* or *well?* Are you tired of stammering your way through the English language? Would you rather be right than hesitant?

There must be many more questions that bother you, that you feel insecure about. The answers to all these questions and many, many more will be found in this book.

You can begin with the following questions yourself. Step right up and try your skill. A series of parallel sentences follows. Each sentence is correct for its own meaning. Each would be wrong if the other meaning were intended. Notice that though there may be only a *slight* difference in appearance, there is sometimes a *vast* difference in meaning.

## DOES IT MAKE ANY DIFFERENCE TO YOU?

(Answers will be found on page 243, but try your skill first.)

### A. THE RIGHT WORD—USAGE, GRAMMAR, SPELLING

1. In which case has the dog the upper paw?
   *a.* A clever dog knows its master.
   *b.* A clever dog knows it's master.

2. To which question, asked by David Susskind of a panel of photographers, was one of them justified in answering, "She's a lousy photographer"?
   *a.* What do you think of Ingrid Bergman as a photographer?
   *b.* As a photographer, what do you think of Ingrid Bergman?

3. Which might be grounds for divorce?
   *a.* My husband likes golf better than I.
   *b.* My husband likes golf better than me.

4. Which judge seems also to be a philanthropist?
   *a.* Having paid my parking fine, I was dismissed by the judge with a reprimand.
   *b.* Having paid my parking fine, the judge dismissed me with a reprimand.

5. Which dog is definitely not a bloodhound?
   *a.* The dog smells bad.
   *b.* The dog smells badly.

6. Which did the doctor order?
   *a.* A large glass of brandy at this time may affect his recovery.
   *b.* A large glass of brandy at this time may effect his recovery.

7. Who will be able to claim a deduction for charitable contributors?
   *a.* He's done good with the money he inherited.
   *b.* He's done well with the money he inherited.

8. In which case was Joe trying to cash in on his father's prominence?
   *a.* Joe flouted his father's authority.
   *b.* Joe flaunted his father's authority.

9. In which case is the menu entirely superfluous?
   *a.* All of the dishes listed on the menu are not available.
   *b.* Not all of the dishes listed on the menu are available.

10. In which did the sharks have a picnic right on the beach?
   *a.* When the old fisherman in Hemingway's *The Old Man and the Sea* got to shore, the marlin was completely devoured by sharks.
   *b.* When the old fisherman in Hemingway's *The Old Man and the Sea* got to shore, the marlin had been completely devoured by sharks.

11. Which may result in an embarrassing situation?
   *a.* The butler was asked to stand by the door and call the guests names as they arrived.
   *b.* The butler was asked to stand by the door and call the guests' names as they arrived.

12. Which required greater imagination?
   *a.* I lay on the psychiatrist's couch for almost an hour.
   *b.* I lied on the psychiatrist's couch for almost an hour.

13. Will the real Gorgons please stand up?
   *a.* If the Gorgons looked at a person they were turned to stone.
   *b.* If the Gorgons looked at a person he was turned to stone.

14. In which case could you call up Jane by looking in the Manhattan phone book?
   *a.* Jane has lived at the Waldorf Astoria for five years.
   *b.* Jane lived at the Waldorf Astoria for five years.

15. Which statement has a sock in it?
   *a.* It's darned good.
   *b.* It's darned well.

16. Which Joe is the amateur?
    *a.* Joe's better than any professional golfer.
    *b.* Joe's better than any other professional golfer.

17. According to Tennyson, which question might have been asked by a member of the famous Light Brigade at Balaclava?
    *a.* Whom are we to ask?
    *b.* Who are we to ask?

18. In which statement is the Argentinian President accused of being a troublemaker?
    *a.* Whether the Argentinian Communists deliberately chose to cause trouble during a period when they knew their President was going to the United States, or whether the course of events rose to a natural climax is hard to tell.
    *b.* Whether the Argentinian Communists deliberately chose a period when they knew their President was going to the United States to cause trouble, or whether the course of events rose to a natural climax is hard to tell.

19. Which sounds somewhat conspiratorial?
    *a.* We'd like to invite you to dessert with us tomorrow evening.
    *b.* We'd like to invite you to desert with us tomorrow evening.

20. In which was the legendary bowman surprisingly careless?
    *a.* Robin Hood was about to loose an arrow.
    *b.* Robin Hood was about to lose an arrow.

## B. COMMAS, SEMICOLONS, AND OTHER MARKS

1. Which is a libel on the fair sex?
    *a.* Thirteen girls knew the secret, all told.
    *b.* Thirteen girls knew the secret; all told.

2. Which sentence shows extraordinary powers of persuasion?
   *a.* I left him convinced he was a fool.
   *b.* I left him, convinced he was a fool.

3. Which convict has a hollow leg?
   *a.* The escaping convict dropped a bullet in his leg.
   *b.* The escaping convict dropped, a bullet in his leg.

4. Which is a denial that politics had anything to do with his appointment?
   *a.* Joe didn't get the appointment, because he is a Republican.
   *b.* Joe didn't get the appointment because he is a Republican.

5. Which makes a foursome?
   *a.* Henry James and I will play with the golf pro tomorrow.
   *b.* Henry, James, and I will play with the golf pro tomorrow.

6. Which is the dedication of a self-confessed polygamist?
   *a.* I dedicate this book to my wife, Edith, for telling me what to leave out.
   *b.* I dedicate this book to my wife Edith for telling me what to leave out.

7. Which refers specifically to the Trojan Horse?
   *a.* Beware the gift bearing Greeks.
   *b.* Beware the gift-bearing Greeks.

8. Which is more flattering to Mrs. Grant?
   *a.* Mrs. Grant is a pretty generous woman.
   *b.* Mrs. Grant is a pretty, generous woman.

9. In which case is Mr. Rogers likely to be bawled out?
   *a.* Mr. Rogers, the secretary is two hours late.
   *b.* Mr. Rogers, the secretary, is two hours late.

10. Which suggests that keeping your cool is profitable?
   *a.* He remained calm, cool, and collected.
   *b.* He remained calm, cool—and collected.

11. In which sentence are you sure that "somatic" and "bodily" mean the same?
   *a.* Radioactive materials that cause somatic, or bodily, damage are to be limited in their use.
   *b.* Radioactive materials that cause somatic or bodily damage are to be limited in their use.

12. Which expresses sincere regret?
   *a.* I'm sorry you can't come with us.
   *b.* I'm sorry. You can't come with us.

13. Which indicates that there were only two people in the car?
   *a.* The two passengers who were seriously hurt were taken to a nearby hospital.
   *b.* The two passengers, who were seriously hurt, were taken to a nearby hospital.

14. In which sentence does the scientist imply he is not frightened?
   *a.* What great scientist recently wrote an article beginning with the three-word sentence, "I am frightened?"
   *b.* What great scientist recently wrote an article beginning with the three-word sentence, "I am frightened"?

15. Which headline is unfair to 8,000,000 people?
   *a.* POPULATION OF NEW YORK CITY BROKEN DOWN BY AGE AND SEX.
   *b.* POPULATION OF NEW YORK CITY, BROKEN DOWN BY AGE AND SEX.

You will have another chance at these pairs of sentences when they appear in the chapters where the particular problem is discussed.

## DON'T FEEL TOO SELF-CONSCIOUS

We all make an occasional error. Discussing the trade of writing, John Mason Brown, who was such a brilliant and effective writer and speaker, had this to say: "One trembles to think how many of us whose profession is writing would be flogged today if lapses in English, or American, were whippable offenses."*

Finally, most of the sentences in this book used as examples of faulty usage or as exercises are taken from the pages of reputable newspapers, magazines, and books! You'll recognize the few that are the homemade variety.

Do you feel better now?

---

* A famous British writer on usage cautions his readers to use the *self* pronouns (*myself, himself, themselves,* etc.) only reflexively, "as in 'I hurt *myself,*' or emphatically, as in 'He, *himself,* did not know. . . .'" But on page 22 of the same book the author writes: "After the felicities of Mr. Empson and Mr. Whitaker, it is a sad decline to pass to some particular example collected by myself. . . ."

Why not, to quote the author against himself (reflexively), simply "collected by me"?

Chapter 2

# The Precision Tools of Speech

> MGM's Director of Motion Picture Research polled the movie-going public to see whether it liked its movie advertising with or without adjectives. The result was interesting: 39 percent of the movie-goers asked, "What are adjectives?"
>
> —*New York Post*

We laugh at the young couple who frantically began taking French lessons in order to be able to understand what their adopted French baby would say when it began to talk. For we know we are not born with any ready-made language.

The first human beings, like animals, probably made sounds which, like the bark of a dog, indicated excitement; or, like the purr of a kitten, expressed contentment; or, like the chatter of monkeys, showed annoyance. Then, man must have been what Tennyson said he still is:

> An infant crying in the night;
> An infant crying for the light,
> And with no language but a cry.

Nature gave man the ability to make these cries as she gave him hands. But just as man had to make tools out of stone and wood to extend the power of his hands, because he found his hands alone too feeble to conquer the earth and wrest from nature what he needed, so he had somehow to invent words, tools made from sound, to take the place of gestures that served so feebly to communicate his needs and express his desires.

And one day the miracle happened. What a great day it was when man began to talk—when the airwaves carried sounds which carried *meaning!* All nature must have smiled with the pride of a doting parent. Junior had uttered his first word!

The various theories of how language began are merely speculative whistlings in the dark—a dark that can never reveal any records to prove or to disprove any of them.

All we know with certainty is that a long, long time ago, man invented an efficient, flexible tool made out of sound. All we can say with certainty is that the invention of radio and television was a lesser miracle.

## NAMES

"And Adam gave names to all cattle, and to the fowl of the air, and to every beast of the field. . . ."

Primitive man named many more things than Adam did. He named *trees* and *stones* and *fruits* and *birds.* He gave names to people about him; those who fed their young were *father* and *mother;* those who were fed were *son* and *daughter.* He named, too, feelings within him: that which made him tremble and run was *fear;* that which made him fight this fear and stirred him to action was *courage.*

All these names of people and things that exist in space or within the experience and heart and mind of man are called NOUNS, a word that means *names.*

## ACTION!

But you can't tell stories with nouns. Nothing happens when you use only nouns. And when nothing happens you have no story. But things *were* happening and man wanted to tell about them. Trees *grew*. Men *killed*. Tribes *hunted*. Birds *sang*.

These words of action are called VERBS. Verbs tell what the noun does or what happens to it or what it is. (Some verbs, such as *is, becomes, appears, seems,* etc., do not show action. These are discussed on page 67.) With them a noun takes wing—a thought is born—a story can be told.

Our newspapers in their headlines can and do use *nouns* and *verbs* to tell their story:

METS CLINCH PENNANT

SENATE ENDS FILIBUSTER

EARTHQUAKE DESTROYS VILLAGE

A noun tells us the SUBJECT that is being talked about. Sometimes, as above, a noun completes the idea contained in the verb and is called the OBJECT. This is the normal thought order: a subject, an action, a receiver of the action (the object).

Indians in Hollywood productions, or anyone trying to use a foreign language, or children in all languages use and understand sentences containing only nouns and verbs: *Chief smoke pipe. Want food. Mamma spank!*

## INFORMATION, PLEASE!

Nouns and verbs expressed complete thoughts, but apparently man was not entirely satisfied. He wanted to boast to others about the one that got away. It wasn't just a fish.

And gestures in such a case were altogether inadequate. No man's reach is as long as his imagination. He needed a word like *tremendous, enormous, gigantic, colossal.* Such words give us more definite information about nouns. Words that give us information about nouns are called ADJECTIVES.

Man also knew that to bring down a deer you had to aim *accurately.* To make sure you didn't scare it away, you had to walk *carefully* and *silently.* The words *accurately, carefully,* and *silently* give us more definite information about the actions of the verbs. They are called ADVERBS. They frequently tell us the *where, when, how,* or *why* of the action.

ADJECTIVES and ADVERBS, therefore, perform the same duty in a sentence: they give information. (In technical language they are called MODIFIERS because they are said to MODIFY, change, or qualify the meanings of other words.) But while adjectives are always tied to some noun's apron strings, adverbs may give us information not only about verbs but about adjectives or other adverbs as well.

She was a *remarkably* pretty girl.

(*Remarkably*—an adverb—gives us information about *pretty,* which is an adjective giving us information about *girl.*)

He ran *unbelievably* fast.

(*Unbelievably*—an adverb—gives us information about *fast,* which is an adverb itself giving us information about *ran.*)

## TIMESAVERS

Somewhere during the development of language the need for timesaving words arose.

It saved time, for instance, to say: "The man caught *and* ate the fish" instead of: "The man caught the fish. The man ate the fish." It saved time to say: "The bear is *under* the tall tree *near* the river" instead of: "See the bear. See the tall tree. See the river."

These shortcut words—*and, under, near*—are connecting words. They are of two kinds.

Those like *near* and *under* are called PREPOSITIONS. The nine prepositions most frequently used are *of, in, to, for, at, from, on, with,* and *by.* They have a very special duty. They *always* connect a noun or a pronoun with some other word in the sentence. They always form a PHRASE with some noun or pronoun:

*under* the tall *tree*
*near* the *river*

When any of these words are used alone, they are no longer prepositions. In the sentence: "The man walked *in,*" *in* is not a connecting word. It is a word giving information about *walked,* and is therefore an adverb.

The other connecting words are called CONJUNCTIONS. There are two kinds. The conjunctions *and, or, but,* and *nor* always connect equal things—two or more nouns or verbs, phrases, and even sentences. They are called coordinate conjunctions.

The other conjunctions, of which there are many (*if, as, when, where, because, although, since, while,* etc.), are called subordinate conjunctions because they always connect a less important statement with the main part of the sentence. If you place any one of these conjunctions in front of the sentence *I see you,* it immediately destroys its independence. *If I see you, when I see you, etc.* are no longer independent sentences. They remain suspended until they are attached to an independent or main clause. For example: *If I see you, I'll tell you.* The suspense is over. We now have the complete statement.

PRONOUNS, which act as substitutes for nouns, are also timesaving words. Instead of repeating the same noun over and over again, we use *he* or *she* or *it*.

## THE COMPLETE PICTURE

Now let's see what we have.

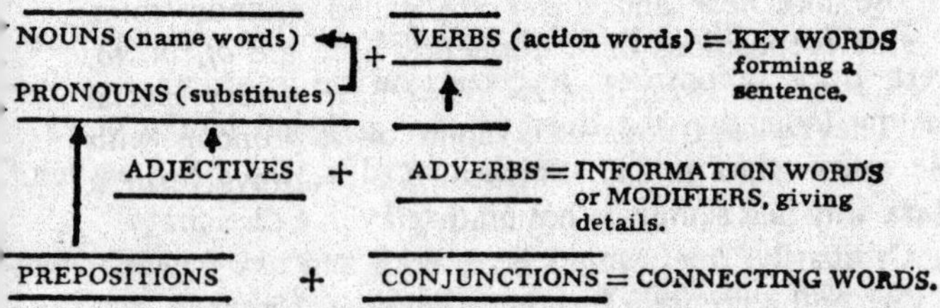


And there you have them—the parts of speech. That's all there is to it.

And here they are all over again in an old-fashioned rhyme, dating back to a time when children threw their heads back and took their grammar—straight!

### GRAMMAR IN RHYME

A NOUN's the name of anything,
As, *school* or *garden, hoop,* or *swing.*

ADJECTIVES tell the kind of noun;
As, *great, small, pretty, white,* or *brown.*

Instead of nouns the PRONOUNS stand:
*Their* heads, *your* face, *its* paw, *his* hand.

VERBS tell of something being done:
You *read, count, sing, laugh, jump,* or *run.*

How things are done the ADVERBS tell;
As, *slowly, quickly, ill,* or *well.*

CONJUNCTIONS join the words together;
As, men *and* women, wind *or* weather.

The PREPOSITION stands before
A noun; as, *in* or *through* a door.

The INTERJECTION shows surprise;
As, *oh!* how pretty! *ah!* how wise!

## WORDS ON DUTY

When a dictionary tells you that a word is a noun or a verb or a preposition it gives you no guarantee. It is merely indicating the duty usually assigned to the word. We know what part of speech a word is *only* when we see it on duty in a sentence, not on display in a dictionary.

Ordinarily, *begs* would be a verb and *ask it* would be a verb and a pronoun forming a complete sentence. Yet see what happens when we look at these words on duty in this clever definition:

> "A community chest is an organization that puts all its *begs* in one *ask-it.*"

Both have become nouns, the names of things!

This is a tricky sentence, of course. But the tricky sentences teach us just as much and they're much more fun. Here are some more. We'll do the first one together.

What part of speech would you call each of the *downs* in the following sentence that might have been taken right off the airwaves?

> "Russell and Hughes of Tech *down* (a) the kick halfway *down* (b) the field, and it's first *down* (c) for Aggie at midfield; and remember, folks, you can come *down* (d) to our store and with a *down* (e) payment of only one dollar you can get one of our new. . . ."

(a) *down* tells what Russell and Hughes did; therefore *down* is a verb.

(b) *down* is a part of the phrase *down the field,* controlling the noun *field,* and is therefore a preposition.

(c) *down* is the name of a situation in football and is therefore a noun. (You can always recognize a noun if you find—or can put—an *a* [*an*] or *the* in front of it.)

(d) *down* tells you *where* to come, describing the action of the verb and is therefore an adverb.

(e) *down* gives us information about *payment,* which is a noun, and is therefore an adjective.

And so we have the word *down* used as five different parts of speech!

Here are some more for you to figure out yourself.

## SELF-QUIZ

1. He was *brave* (a), for none but the *brave* (b) can *brave* (c) the violence of the sea.

2. He was accustomed to read his *daily* (a) while swallowing his *daily* (b) breakfast of orange juice, toast, and tea, as well as the pill he took three times *daily* (c).

3. In their rage they *stone* (a) the man, who is *stone* (b) deaf, with a *stone* (c) taken from the *stone* (d) wall.

4. The talk went *round* (a) the *round* (b) table as the members of the panel had another *round* (c) of drinks to help them continue the discussion *round* (d) the clock.

5. I certainly *object* (a) when the *object* (b) of my affections tries to give me an *object* (c) lesson in public.

6. We must expect to go slowly, *for* (a) this is a problem that has vexed mankind *for* (b) ages.

7. *In* (a) the auditorium were many people who had gone *in* (b) without paying, because they have an "*in*" (c) with the management.

8. *Present* (a) plans call for a farewell *present* (b) that we *present* (c) to him with everyone *present* (d).

9. We usually *light* (a) the corridor, which is not always very *light* (b), with a *light* (c) that is covered with a *light* (d) green shade.

10. "*Well!* (a)" he exclaimed, "I am *well* (b) and I have done *well* (c)."

## WORD FORMATION

Not very much would get done in a repair shop if a mechanic yelled over to his assistant, "Hey, Joe, let me have a whatsis to fasten this doohickey onto the whatcha-ma-call-it."

Just as one must learn the precise vocabulary of one's trade or profession, so it is necessary for you to learn the names of and recognize the different "doodads" that constitute the parts of a sentence.

In these exercises you are to change the given word to as many other parts of speech as you can. Words ending in *ing, er, or,* or *ist* are not acceptable.

In the first exercise you are to change the form given —a verb—to three other parts of speech in the same family and to label each one as the dictionary does: v, n, adj, adv.

Example: differ (v), difference (n), different (adj), differently (adv)

### A

1. compare
2. confide
3. destroy
4. describe
5. deceive
6. defy
7. exclude
8. analyze
9. resent
10. subvert

B.

(Here you begin with a noun. Sometimes you can change it to three other parts of speech, sometimes to only two.)

1. accident
2. beauty
3. democracy
4. grammar
5. miracle
6. mischief
7. omen
8. chaos
9. apology
10. prophecy

C.

(Here you begin with an adjective. Sometimes you can change it to only one other part of speech. But there are two or even three possibilities for most of them.)

1. generous
2. efficient
3. formal
4. frivolous
5. lonely
6. sincere
7. similar
8. humid
9. immune
10. immobile

D.

(These are some difficult words combining all three [A, B, and C] we've already done. Remember to label each form as v., n., adj., or adv. Sometimes you will be able to change a word to only one other part of speech.)

1. unanimous
2. hypocrisy
3. tragedy
4. crux
5. contend
6. curious
7. enjoin
8. jeopardy
9. portent
10. remedy
11. ecstasy
12. ambiguous
13. pious
14. joke
15. miscellany
16. climax
17. apathy
18. space
19. circumstance
20. prodigy

Chapter 3

# What Is the Mistake Most Often Made?

> After some twenty years of lint picking, W & S* is in a position to say that the grammatical error that crops up in the paper most often is disagreement between subject and verb. This sort of thing: "More independence and initiative in agricultural planning was given today to the farmers. . . ." Or this sort: ". . . the Egyptian version of his remarks were published."
>
> —THEODORE M. BERNSTEIN

## PRETEST ON THE MISTAKE MOST OFTEN MADE

Choose the verb in parentheses that you think agrees with the subject in number.

1. Insofar as the treatment of war prisoners (is, are) concerned, let me make this perfectly clear.

2. He estimated that one out of ten high-stake games (was, were) played with a marked deck.

3. (There's, There are) bound to be inequities no matter how the draft is run.

4. Scarcely a hundred yards away—across the canal—(was, were) an Egyptian officer and three soldiers.

---

* W & S is "Winners and Sinners," a bright and witty bulletin of second-guessing issued occasionally by Theodore M. Bernstein, assistant manager of *The New York Times* until the end of 1969, now editorial director of the New York Times Book Division. Mr. Bernstein is the author of *Watch Your Language, The Careful Writer,* and *Miss Thistlebottom's Hobgoblins.*

5. A high school diploma or its equivalent (is, are) required for entrance to certain courses.

6. Neither snow nor rain nor heat nor gloom of night (stays, stay) these couriers from the swift completion of their appointed rounds.

7. *The New York Times,* together with other New York papers, (has, have) been trying to reach a settlement with the Mailers Union No. 6.

8. There (was, were), of course, some effective blocking, some nice faking and passing, and some good running.

9. What other steps can be taken in that direction (is, are) being discussed by the steering group in Washington.

10. About the only thing you can get for a nickel these days (is, are) five pennies.

11. Nor is it I who (has, have) ever proposed that we negotiate from a position of weakness.

12. The three astronauts (was, were) in a very cheerful mood.

In sentence 12 you didn't have to think for even a second. Your ear let you know at once. The harmony was pleasing.

No educated person would say (or write): "They was here" or "He are a fine fellow." In all these cases the verb *immediately follows* its subject and there's no problem.

But there are times when the verb does not immediately follow, and there are times when the verb precedes the subject noun or pronoun. Then even writers may sometimes be trapped. Let's look at the traps in each of the first eleven sentences.

In numbers 1 and 2 there are *words between* the subject and the verb, and your ear is fooled. In number 1, *treatment* is the subject and *of war prisoners* is an intervening prepositional phrase. In number 2, *one* is the subject and *out of ten high-stake games* is again an intervening phrase. You have to cut away the intervening words and strip the sentence down to the real subject.

In numbers 3, 4, and 8 the verb *precedes* the subject (it always does in sentences that begin with *there*). What you do here is to read the sentence without the word *there* (or in 4 without the introductory phrase) and you have: 3: "inequities *are* bound to be," 4: "an Egyptian officer and three soldiers *were*," and 8: "some effective blocking, some nice faking and passing, and some good running *were*."

In numbers 5 and 6 the two or more subjects are connected not by *and* which produces a plural but by *or* and *nor* which separate. In such cases you ignore everything but the last in the series and so you read—5: "its equivalent *is* required" and 6: "gloom of night *stays*." When subjects are connected by *or* and *nor*, the number of the verb is determined by the noun that *immediately* precedes it. For example, take these two sentences:

*"Either you boys or I am going to be in charge,"* or *"Either I or you boys are going to be in charge."**

In 7, even though "together with other New York papers" seems to add to the subject, grammar recognizes only *and* as an additive. The others, like *together with, along with, in addition to, as well as,* etc., are regarded as merely intervening phrases.

In 9 the subject is the entire clause *what other steps can be taken in that direction,* one unit and therefore singular.

In 10, you may be tempted to use *are* because it is followed by *five pennies,* but the subject is *thing.*

In 11, *who* is a substitute for *I* and you would say *I have,* not *I has;* therefore *who have.*

---

* When *neither* and *nor* are involved, many writers use the plural form in all cases. Grammatically, however, one should write, "Neither the colonel nor the captain WAS ready to talk."

Now that you know, try these. Be sure to strip each sentence down to the real subject and verb when the verb *follows*. Be sure to reverse the sentence when the verb *precedes*. Remember only *and* adds, and therefore makes a plural.

EXERCISE A

1. The senator, like the others, (was, were) shaking every hand within reach.

2. The power and the presence of the commando movement (has, have) mushroomed in the last four years.

3. The discharge of industrial wastes (create, creates) a situation that must be corrected now.

4. (Is, Are) the strategy and the tactics of the two brothers actually counterproductive to the cause of peace?

5. During the eclipse one of the two things astronomers will look for (is, are) comets.

6. The use of these facilities (has, have) increased greatly in the past year.

7. The new model as well as several older models (is, are) included in the sale.

8. The slum districts of any large city in this country or any other country (breed, breeds) crime and disease.

9. The loss of eight helicopters (was, were) announced in an official communiqué.

10. Neither of the two women (was, were) named in the bomb-plot indictment.

11. Around the corner on the left (is, are) a theater and a public library.

12. The value of these daily exercises (lie, lies) in their being suitable for people of all ages.

13. In any enterprise (there's, there are) many things to be considered.

14. Any notions of racial superiority or purity (is, are) definitely refuted by science.

15. Pollution of the air, the water, and the land (threaten, threatens) to undo the advances of science.

16. The main target of the President's remarks (was, were) what he called the neo-isolationists.

17. Once there (was, were) Banzhof and Nader; now there (is, are) hosts of consumer activists.

18. Neither of these shows (is, are) exceptional, but both painters make the most of their virtues.

19. A person's actions during a crisis in his life (is, are) influenced by his basic character.

20. How many liters of oxygen (is, are) required for complete combustion?

21. The color of his eyes (is, are) blue.

22. The basis for all these laws (is, are) prejudice and hypocrisy.

23. Either you or the previous borrower (doesn't, don't) care very much about public property.

24. Is he so politically naïve that he thinks the butcher, the baker, or the candlestick-maker still (run, runs) for public office?

25. Time for recruitment and adequate training (is, are) needed.

## A DEMURRER OR TWO

Even to the cultivated ear a compound (therefore plural) subject after *there's* often seems in tune. *There's some ice cream and a piece of apple pie in the refrigerator* doesn't jar the ear. Indeed it pleases, as compared with the rather stuffy *There are some ice cream and a piece of apple pie in the refrigerator,* which is grammatically correct. However, in the sentence *(There's, There are) three possibilities,* the word *are* is the only form to use.

A good suggestion is to use *there* less often. For instance, *You will find some ice cream and a piece of apple pie in the refrigerator* doesn't lead to the kind of awkward construction that you get involved in with *there.*

I have before me a sentence from David Schoenbrunn's review of *We the Vietnamese:* "What is their history, their religion, their customs, their way of life, their culture?"

Would anyone fault him for not using *are* to take care of the five individual nouns? Would you want to begin with *What are* in this particular case when each subject is insulated by commas? That doesn't mean you never say *What are.* In *What are your plans for the weekend?,* the verb *are* is compulsory. But in the Schoenbrunn sentence, sound and style push aside strict grammatical considerations.

## FINE POINTS

### The Intervening Phrase

The noun in the phrase that intervenes between the subject and the verb does in certain cases determine the number of the verb.

Whenever the intervening phrase between the subject and the verb is equivalent to MANY or SOME, a plural verb is used.

> Half of the apples (many) WERE spoiled.
> A lot of people (many) ARE beginning to speak up.
> A variety of prizes (many) WERE offered.

BUT

> Half of the crop (much) WAS spoiled.
> A lot of work (much) IS still needed.

We see that in such cases the noun following the word *of* determines the choice of the verb. Your ear would direct you correctly, anyhow.

### NOW TRY THESE

1. Involved in the research (was, were) all manner of creatures from men and monkeys to rats and mice, goldfish, flatworms, and Japanese quail.

2. A lot of the action (is, are) effectively filmed in black and white.

3. A variety of bacteria (is, are) helpful in the digestive process.

4. There (was, were) a lot of tramps on the road.

5. One-third of the regiment (was, were) wounded.

6. One-third of the soldiers (was, were) wounded.

7. A lot of trouble (was, were) avoided.

8. A number of students (is, are) picketing the embassy.

## THE WORD **NUMBER**

The word *number* behaves in what seems to be a peculiar fashion.

*The number* followed by a plural phrase takes a verb in the singular, as for example:

> The number of polluted rivers and lakes *has* increased.

*A number* followed by a plural phrase takes a verb in the plural, as in:

> A number of ways of fighting pollution *have* been suggested.

Why is this so? Perhaps because in the first sentence the word *number* is statistical (i.e., the number is important), whereas in the second sentence you can substitute *many* for *a number*.

### TRY THESE

1. A number of displaced civilians (was, were) willing to leave their country forever.

2. The total number of full-time freshmen on all campuses (was, were) estimated to be 1.63 million.

3. An increasing number of recruits (is, are) bringing their civilian-acquired addictions with them to this training center.

## COLLECTIVE NOUNS

For nouns like *government, public, management,* etc., the British favor the plural. It is always *The government are.* In the United States we prefer *The government is.* We use the singular verb unless there is evidence within the sentence that the members making up the group are being considered as individuals.

1. Joe's family was always quarreling.
2. Joe's family were always quarreling.

Both sentences are right, but the first one seems to say that Joe's family, as a unit, quarrels with the Joneses or the Smiths. The second seems to imply that the individual members of Joe's family quarrel among themselves.

With words that end in *s* in the singular or plural form of the noun, like *politics, ethics. mathematics,* we can apply the same test.

> The theme of the book roughly is that politics is the art of the possible.

"My politics are not yours, Senator, but I like what you say."

(Here *politics* equals *political beliefs* or *acts.*)

### EXERCISE B

1. Politics (is, are) a career that has attracted many lawyers.

2. The politics of those on trial (is, are) not in question.

3. His ethics (is, are) in need of overhauling.

4. Ethics (is, are) a branch of philosophy.

5. Athletics (is, are) his chief interest.

### One or More?

Horace Greeley, who always insisted that the word *news* was plural, once wired to his star reporter: ARE THERE ANY NEWS? The reply came back promptly: NOT A NEW.

There are many words ending in *s* that have peculiar habits.

Some, though they may refer to only *one* thing, are rarely used in the singular: *scissors, pincers, trousers, pants,* for instance.

No one would say, "My trousers is hanging in the closet."

## WHICH, WHO, AND THAT

In which is money the root of love?

*a.* The great rich Miss Crawley, whom her two brothers adore, has arrived with her £70,000.

*b.* The great, rich Miss Crawley has arrived with her £70,000, which her two brothers adore.
(Adapted from Thackeray's *Vanity Fair*)

It can be seen from the above that *which* refers to things and *who* to persons. *That* may refer to either. More will be said about the use of *that* in the chapter on punctuation, page 203. It is sufficient to say here that *who* and *which* are either singular or plural depending on their antecedents. We say *Boys who are* and *A boy who is;* we say *Stones that* (or *which*) *are thrown* or *A stone that* (or *which*) *is thrown. I, who am never late, overslept. My friend, you who are always so sure, I have news for you.* There's not much of a problem there.

The controversy occurs when *one of* is used. For example, in *He is one of the writers who has*—or is it *have?—been officially barred.* Grammatically, we can see that *who* refers to *writers,* which is plural, and *have* should be used.

But there is an easier way to tell without using grammar. Whenever one of these sentences appears, begin reading the sentence at the word *of. Of the writers who have*—it couldn't be *has—been barred, he is one.* Your ear tells you that. If you want to argue that *who* really tells you about *he* and you use *has,* don't worry about it. It's not that important.

Just for practice, then, do these, remembering to begin reading the sentence at the word *of* in solving the problem.

## LOOK, MA, NO GRAMMAR

1. Mr. Smith is one *of the writers who* (has, have) *been officially barred.*

2. Handel's "Saul" is one *of those works that* (has, have) *remained in limbo,* not quite forgotten but probably never performed entire.

3. This ballet company possesses one *of the greatest choreographers who* (has, have) *ever lived.*

4. I'm one *of those people who* (thinks, think) *it necessary to act*—and act soon.

5. Ben Shahn's pen-and-ink drawing "Safe" is one *of several works that* (uses, use) *baseball as their subjects.*

6. Are you one *of the 2,000,000 people who* (is, are) *going to buy a compact car this year?*

7. This is one of *those novels that* (deal, deals) *with the generation gap.*

8. Private Jones was one *of the recruits who thought* (himself, themselves) *mistreated.*

## FOREIGN PLURALS

There are a few words taken over from Latin and Greek that still retain their original plurals. In some cases we can use either. *Formulas* is seen more often than *formulae*, but *addenda, stimuli,* and *criteria* are found more often than *addendums, stimuluses*, and *criterions.*

However, one must exercise some care to distinguish between the singular and plural form. The returning alumnus who greeted a former professor with, "Don't you remember me? I'm an alumni," was properly put in his place when the professor rejoined with, "How singular!"

It's a touchy business. Many think that *media, strata, bacteria,* and *phenomena* are all singular. They aren't. By sheer force of usage *agenda* and *insignia* have become singular. *Data,* a plural, is used both ways.

In a recent best seller, *The Andromeda Strain,* I came upon these two sentences:

> Perhaps it [intelligent life on a distant planet] was no larger than a *bacterium.* (p. 127 in the paperback)

> Take up a harmless *bacteria* and bring it back in a new form virulent and unexpected. (p. 133)

So there you are! And here if you're interested are some foreign singular and plural forms of words often used in English. (An *i* ending is pronounced *eye;* an *ae* ending, *ee.*)

> LATIN: algae (plural, pronounced aljee); dictum, dicta; effluvium, effluvia; erratum, errata; medium (a means of mass communication), media; stimulus, stimuli; stratum, strata.

The following have the normal English plural as well as the Latin: Those ending in *us* have the *i* plural; those ending in *um* have the *a* plural: cactus, fungus (*j* sound in *fungi*), nucleus, curriculum, memorandum.

> GREEK: Words ending in *is* form their plurals by changing *is* to *es* (pronounced *eez*): analysis, crisis, hypothesis, oasis, synopsis, thesis. Words ending in *on* form their plurals by changing *on* to *a:* criterion, criteria; phenomenon, phenomena.
>
> HEBREW: Plural is formed by adding *im:* kibbutz, kibbutzim. (The last syllable, *tseem,* is accented.)

All of the following sentences were either uttered by famous men or written in well-known newspapers, and in every case the form selected for the foreign word was wrong. The word is easily identified. You are to supply the proper ending.

1. One great lesson of this *phenomen. . .* is that the world will not live in harmony so long as two-thirds of its inhabitants find it difficult to live at all.

2. A different *criteri. . .* applies in this case.

3. Now television is also becoming a *medi. . .* of mounting importance to religion.

4. The agency represents over 200 *kibbutz*. . . throughout Israel.

5. Therein lies the controversy cutting across every *strat*. . . of society.

6. They have developed a *bacteri*. . . which may combat bubonic plague.

GRAMMAR ON POSTCARD

TO THE EDITOR OF THE NEW YORK TIMES:

Recently, in common with all other registered voters in this city, I received from the Board of Elections a form postcard mailed out for the announced purpose of discovering whether my "name and address is correct * * *." I was delighted to be able to inform the board that they certainly is.

ROBERT J. CAHN

## Chapter 4

# The Case of the Elusive Pronouns

> But it's on the talk shows that careless grammar runs rampant. I have heard David Frost, no less, say several times to a guest, "I'm sure our next guest will be entertaining for you and I." Nice language for an Englishman.
>
> And John Connally, our Secretary of the Treasury, in one interview said twice, "If a person invests their money in municipal bonds. . . ."
>
> Added to these are the countless "papers laying on the floor," and "between you and I," and "Who, in your opinion, will the Democrats pick to run for President?" Ad nauseam.
>
> —From "Top of My Head"
> by GOODMAN ACE,
> *Saturday Review,* April 17, 1971

The case of the elusive pronouns sounds like a mystery story. It isn't. There's no mystery. It's easy if you don't use grammar to solve it. That's right. No grammar.

Just to prove my point we'll tackle the mystery of *who–whom* first. Faced with a choice of *who* or *whom,* even seasoned writers hesitate and finally plunge in blindly.

But while it's still a mystery, try this pretest and see how well you can solve it *your* way.

### PRETEST

1. Intelligent citizens will vote for (whoever, whomever) they think is best qualified.

2. (Who, Whom) shall I say is calling?

3. He is the one (who, whom) I'd like to see win the election.

4. Stevenson, like Bayh, pointed to the other 75 men (who, whom) he said were serving terms for murder in Vietnam.

5. Private sources have offered $100,000 reward for information leading to the arrest of (whoever, whomever) it was who bombed the Capitol a week ago.

6. However, he had kind words for all the Republican prospects and promised to support (whoever, whomever) was chosen.

7. The Manhattan and Bronx organizations were asked to pledge their support to (whoever, whomever) wins the Democratic election.

8. It gives me great pleasure to nominate a man (who, whom) all of us know to be the best fitted for the job.

9. The security police are rounding up persons (who, whom) it is suspected might do harm to the State.

10. It was the same tall, heavy infantry officer (who, whom) we had seen double-timing it into the building a few minutes before.

## YOU CAN DO IT BETTER WITHOUT GRAMMAR

If you used grammar in the first sentence of the pretest, you might have fallen into the trap of thinking that *who–whom* was either the object of the preposition *for* or the following verb *think*.

The nongrammatical approach has no pitfalls: you win every time, and it's as easy as 1, 2, 3.

Here are the three simple steps:

*Step 1.* Consider ONLY the words that FOLLOW *who* or *whom*. In sentence 1, you would then be left with:

> *they think     is best qualified.*

*Step 2.* You can see that there's a gap in the thought. Plug the gap with either *he* or *him*, whichever makes sense and you get:

> *they think* HE *is best qualified.*

*Step 3.* Now apply a simple formula: he = who; him = whom:

> Solution: *Intelligent citizens will vote for* WHOEVER *they think is best qualified.*

Easy? Yes.

Let's work out sentence 3 of the pretest together:

*Step 1:* The words that follow *who* or *whom* are:

> *I'd like to see     win the election.*

*Step 2:* Plug the gap:

> *I'd like to see* HIM *win the election.*

*Step 3:* him = whom:

> Solution: *He is the one* WHOM *I'd like to see win the election.*

Now go back to the pretest and practice the three steps. You can be sure of the correct answers without looking for them on page 245.

## NOW TRY THESE

All of these sentences are taken from the writings of well-known journalists or famous authors of books. And all of them made the wrong choice between *who* or *whom!* You won't—if you use the three steps. You will get *all* of them right.

1. In his introduction, he speaks of Mr. Kazantzakis (who, whom) many consider to be one of the great writers of our time.

2. I am fortunate enough to be married to a fashion-conscious man (who, whom) I think has infallible taste.

3. She castigated the Unionist politicians (who, whom) she said fostered religious hatred for their own ends.

4. Bernard Shaw once wrote: "No! I lay an eternal curse on (whosoever, whomsoever) shall now or at any time hereafter make schoolbooks of my works and make me hated as Shakespeare is hated."

5. (Whoever, Whomever) it may be, the new coach will be on hand for the Tarpons' spring practice.

6. Deborah Kerr plays the wife of an American businessman in London (who, whom) she grows to suspect is an uncaught murderer.

7. They are making a serious effort now to translate most writers (who, whom) they think reach a high standard.

8. He told the audience (who, whom) he thought was responsible for the Credibility Gap.

9. In the film she arrives at the villa of her father (who, whom) she hasn't seen in a long time.

10. She had a beautiful daughter (who, whom) she hoped would rise to success.

11. She met the Baron (who, whom) she knew had many acquaintances among emigré Russian nobility.

12. The man (who, whom) real estate men call Bill is in debt to numerous creditors.

13. The Governor said only that he would vote for (whoever, whomever) would be the Republican Convention nominee.

14. The award is given to the performer (who, whom) *Cue* editors believe showed the greatest achievement in the year just past.

15. The lyrics are by Johnny Brandon, (who, whom) I take to be British.

Now that you've gone through all the trouble of deciding between *who* and *whom,* let me tell you that you're almost always safe with *who.* For centuries famous writers have been using sentences like "*Who* was the article written by?" When *who* immediately follows the preposition, as in "By *whom* was the article written?" or "We're trying to locate the people with *whom* the suspect associated while in New York City," your ear prevents you from using *who.*

I once heard a receptionist answering the telephone in a publisher's office ask, "And the message is for Mrs. Whom?" That's going a bit too far. As a matter of fact, in conversation (when you have no opportunity to use the three steps) always use *who.* If I were given to predictions, I would say that in fifty years—give or take five—the only form used will be *who.* After all, *which* is always *which.*

## I OR ME? HE OR HIM? WE OR US? THEY OR THEM?

### PRETEST

(Some sentences that follow are grammatically correct; some are not. Decide whether the words in italics are used correctly.)

1. Last summer my aunt and uncle invited my brother and *me* to their country home.

2. Although I'm two years younger than my brother, I'm just as tall as *him* and much smarter than *him.*

3. When *me* and my brother reached the station, my uncle was there to meet us.

4. In his hand he had two tennis racquets, which he had just bought for my brother and *me.*

5. "You weren't worried about *we* boys, were you, Uncle?" I asked.

6. He put his arms affectionately about my brother and *I* and said, "I let your aunt do all the worrying."

7. Just between you and *I,* my uncle was right.

8. When we arrived at the house, my aunt had changed so much that I wasn't sure it was *she.*

9. My uncle, who always likes his jokes, knocked loudly on the door and called in, "There's nobody here except *us* chickens!"

10. If you were *me,* wouldn't you be very happy too?

Nobody has any trouble when there is only the pronoun involved. Nobody—with any kind of ear—would say:

1. Me saw the man

or

2. The man saw I.

Grammatically, in sentence 1 the pronoun is the subject of the sentence and is therefore in the nominative, or subject, case. In sentence 2, the pronoun is the object of the verb *saw* and is therefore in the objective case *(me).*

There's no problem here. The problem occurs when there are several pronouns linked by *and* or *or,* and your ear is no longer a safe guide.

Let us take these sentences:

1. Me and Bob saw the man

   and

2. The man saw Bob and I.

Your ear doesn't help much. We, therefore, must first strip the sentence down by crossing out the words *and* and *Bob.* We then get

Me saw the man

and

The man saw I.

Now your ear tells you that *I* belongs in sentence 1 and *me* belongs in sentence 2. When we put back the words *and* and *Bob,* we get:

Bob and I saw the man

and

The man saw Bob and me.

It's as easy as that. We just cross out what gets in the way of

## PLAYING IT BY EAR

Now try these sentences. Remember to omit whatever gets in the way so that you reduce each sentence to the pattern of *(I, Me) saw the man* or *The man saw (I, me).* I'll do the crossing out for you in the first two sentences. After that you're on your own.

1. My uncle invited ~~Fred and~~ (I, me) to go on a fishing trip with him.

2. The dean gave some good advice to ~~George and~~ (I, me).

3. (We, Us) boys would rather fight than switch.

4. Bob and (I, me) have been asked to serve as ushers.

5. My father bought a transistor radio for my brother and (I, me).

6. I think they should have told Bob and (he, him) about it.

7. This is a question for you and (they, them) to decide.

8. There was no one at home but Spot and (I, me).

9. I think (we, us) fellows should be allowed in free.

10. I remember my sister and (I, me) standing up in front of the mirror for hours combing our hair.

11. He wrote to us from South Vietnam to pray for (he, him) and his friends.

12. This is something for (we, us) Americans to be proud of.

13. Here is a picture of Jennifer, Daddy, and (I, me).

14. Remember to send along best wishes from my mother and (I, me).

## PRONOUNS AFTER COMPARISONS

For pronouns in comparisons we change our tactics. Instead of crossing out words we add them, completing the words *implied after than or as.*

My brother is taller than (I, me).

The temptation is to use *me,* but if we complete the words after *than* we have *than I (am tall).* It's probably a good idea to do this anyhow. *Than I* seems very bare.

In the paired sentences in Chapter 1 (A 3), it is easy to answer the question if we complete the sentences.

> My husband likes golf better than I (do).
>
> My husband likes golf better than (he does) me.

HERE ARE A FEW TO PLAY AROUND WITH:

1. My friend has always been more fortunate than (I, me).
2. I am not as well informed as (she, her).
3. Do you think he plays as well as (I, me)?
4. We all agreed that no one of our friends was more highly regarded than (he, him).
5. My younger brother is stronger than (I, me).

In this situation, too, usage has put in a strong bid, and the objective forms, *me, him, her, us, them,* are often heard in speech and seen in informal writing.

## PRONOUNS AFTER THE VERB TO BE

You are listening to the broadcast of a baseball game. The Met pitcher is in trouble, the manager is at the mound, and Tug McGraw is warming up in the bullpen. Should the announcer say, "McGraw is ready. The next pitcher will probably be he"? Or should it be *him?*

Red Barber, a stickler for good English, always used to say, "The next pitcher will be he." And *he* is the grammatically correct form. I could give you the grammatical reason and tell you that *he* is the predicate nominative after *will be*. Would that help? So again we are going to solve the problem without grammar.

Here's how. A sentence containing any part of the verb *to be* (*is, was, were, has been, will be*, etc.) is reversible. We can say:

> Tom Seaver is one of baseball's best pitchers.
>
> or
>
> One of baseball's best pitchers is Tom Seaver.

We can say:

> His power is great.
>
> or
>
> Great is his power.

Now let's reverse Red Barber's sentence *The next pitcher will be (he, him)* and see what happens. We certainly wouldn't say *Him will be the next pitcher*. Your ear tells you that that is wrong. Therefore, *The next pitcher will be he* is grammatically correct because when we reverse the sentence we have *He will be the next pitcher*.

## REVERSE ENGLISH

Now try these sentences and remember you get the grammatically correct answer by reversing the part of the sentence that has a part of the verb *to be* in it.

1. I told you it was (she, her). (Notice we reverse only *it was she, her*.)
2. Among the medal winners were Joe and (I, me).
3. The only one at home was (I, me).
4. I could have sworn the guilty one was (he, him).
5. The last one to get back from the party was (she, her).
6. The murderer could not possibly have been (he, him).

7. The persons referred to in the news item were (we, us).

8. We look so much alike that people often take him to be (I, me).

9. He took my brother to be (I, me).

10. At the banquet the guests of honor were my sister and (I, me).

At this point let me put in a word for usage as opposed to grammar. You would sound pretty stuffy if you said, "It's I" or "Who, I?" Some years ago Winston Churchill put his seal of approval on "It's me." Notice that *It is I* is still in general use. Who knows how many years from now *It's him, It's her, It's us, It's them* may go the way of *It's me,* though *It's me* has the further support of the analogy that can be made with the French *C'est moi.*

## THE STRANGE CASE OF "BUT"

*But,* as you know, can be either a conjunction opposed to *and* in meaning or a preposition meaning *except.* In its use as *except* it should normally be followed by the objective case (*me, her, him, us,* etc.), but the ear is really the guide. Take the sentence

> Who *but he* [Noel Coward] has written his own plays and musical comedies, directed them, acted in them, danced in them, and sung in them songs of his own composition?

*But* is a preposition, but to put *him* after *but* and have a sequence such as *but him has written* jars on the ear, and *he* takes over very neatly.

If the *but* phrase comes at the end of a sentence, here in America we usually use the objective case. In England, however, the *but* is construed as a conjunction and the subject, or nominative, case takes over.

> That I suffered in secret and that I suffered exquisitely no one ever knew but I.
>
> (from *David Copperfield*)

We would be inclined in America to write *but me,* as we would write *except me.* Even the colloquial expression is, "There's nobody here but *us* chickens."

## THE POSSESSIVE CASE OF NOUNS AND PRONOUNS

### MOURNING BECOMES THE APOSTROPHE

I fear that I shall never be
Quite sure of the apostrophe.

My brain is addled, I confess;
Does it precede or follow S?

My feeble mind has running fits
When I consider *its* or *it's*.

Now Geoffrey Chaucer never used it
And firmly G.B.S. eschewed it.

Grammarians made the apostrophe,
I think, to harass fools like me!

—EVELYN A. HAMMETT,
from *Word Study*,
February, 1963

1. Which may result in an embarrassing situation?
   *a.* The butler was asked to stand at the door and call the guests names as they arrived.
   *b.* The butler was asked to stand at the door and call the guests' names as they arrived.

2. In which case does the dog have the upper paw?
   *a.* A clever dog knows it's master.
   *b.* A clever dog knows its master.
3. Which is more likely to be a golf stick?
   *a.* A lady's club.
   *b.* A ladies' club.
4. Which is an invitation to some kind of exhibit?
   *a.* We'd like to have you see our students work.
   *b.* We'd like to have you see our students' work.

I'm not going to give you the answers, but I will give you some help. Where the apostrophes appear, I'll explain what they mean:

Pair 1: the guests' names = the names of the guests

Pair 2: it's = it is

Pair 3: a lady's club = a club belonging to a lady
a ladies' club = a club to which ladies belong

Pair 4: our students' work = the work of our students

If you are studying French or Spanish or Italian, you know that those languages always take the long way around. They don't use the apostrophe to show possession: it is always the hat *of my mother,* the guitar *of my uncle,* the house *of my grandmother,* the pen *of my aunt.*

## PRETEST

In the following sentences taken from recent newspapers and magazines, change the words in italics that follow a noun to the possessive form using the apostrophe.

*Example:* This is a symbol of the concern *of the government* for the protection of the rights *of its citizens.*

*Rewritten:* This is a symbol of *the government's* concern for the protection of *its citizens'* rights.

(Notice that by approaching the problem this way, it is easier to tell whether the apostrophe precedes or follows the *s,* one of the problems mentioned in the poem at the beginning of this section.)

1. The Prime Minister *of England* quickly said he would announce the names *of the agitators.*

2. The newspaper *of yesterday* announced a record enrollment of about fifty-six million in the schools *of the nation.*

3. The acoustic tests followed the special matinee *for children.*

4. After the speeches *of the candidates,* a vote was called for.

5. The celebration was held in Portsmouth, birthplace *of Charles Dickens.*

6. The educated guesses *of scientists* on the total number of viruses that cause colds range from one hundred to two hundred.

7. An extraordinary sale of clothes *for men,* hats *for ladies,* and shoes *for children* was announced in the newspaper *of today.*

8. The longest disarmament conference *in history* is winding up its fifth summer.

9. The automobiles *of next year* will cost more than the automobiles *of this year.*

10. It is the aim *of Indian planners* to lift Calcutta to a place as one of the great metropolises *of the world.*

## RULES FOR THE APOSTROPHE IN POSSESSIVES

In the preceding exercise you may have encountered some problems in converting the phrases to possessives. Probably the biggest problem was deciding whether to place the apostrophe before or after the *s*. The rules for placement of the apostrophe are simple. Applying them correctly is sometimes difficult.

1. If a noun—singular or plural—does not end in *s*, add the apostrophe and *s:* boy's, men's, women's.

2. If a plural ends in *s*, there's no problem: you add only the apostrophe after the *s:* boys', families', cars', countries'.

3. If a singular noun or a name ends in *s*, add either *'s* or just an apostrophe. A good rule to follow is to write it the way you pronounce it. If you say "Joneses car," then write *Jones's car;* if you say "the princesses mother," then write *the princess's mother.* (This assumes, of course, that only one princess is involved. If there were more than one princess, you would write the *princesses' mother.*) Since you don't say "for goodnesses sake," write *for goodness' sake.*

A sign on a house in Portsmouth, England, reads:

| Charles Dickens' Birthplace<br>February 7th, 1812 |
|---|

However, the form *Dickens's* is found just as frequently. Thus you were right either way in number 5 in the exercise unless you wrote Charles *Dicken's*. *Dicken's* is obviously wrong, since his last name was not Dicken.

People do have trouble deciding where to put the apostrophe when a noun or name ends in *s*. I know of a butcher shop on Foster Avenue in Brooklyn that was called "Charle's Meat Market," and the newspapers recently showed a picture of a sign over a store which read "Glady's Beauty Shop"!

4. Where the name ending in *s* is long or where there are many *s*'s in the name, it's best to settle for the apostrophe alone:

> Sophocles' seven tragedies, Archimedes' principle, Achilles' strength, Socrates' philosophy

This rule also holds for singular nouns that end in an *s* sound but have no *s*, as in:

> for appearance' sake, for conscience' sake

5. Where there is joint ownership of a single property, only the last name gets the apostrophe, as in:

> Schultz and Murphy's department store, Mary and John's house

But where two people each own similar but separate properties, we say: John's and Bill's golf clubs, Pat's and Sally's dresses.

CAUTION

The possessives of personal pronouns are never indicated by apostrophes. There are no such words as *your's, our's, her's, hi's, their's,* or *its',* although I've seen them around—all but *hi's*.

The word *its* is undoubtedly the most manhandled and misused of all. Even those who should know better misuse this little pronoun. A great airline boasts of *"it's* fine cuisine." A meat-packing house proudly urges us to buy its product because of "*it's* fine quality."

I can categorically state that the word *its* never has an apostrophe. What, never? Yes, never. Because when *its* has an apostrophe, *it's* isn't a word; it is two words, *it* and *is* or *it* and *has*. *A clever dog knows it's master* means that the dog knows that its master no longer has the upper hand.

## EXERCISE IN USE OF THE APOSTROPHE FOR POSSESSIVES

Now you ought to be able to take these in stride. Copy the following sentences, inserting an apostrophe or an *'s* wherever one belongs.

1. Has anyone seen this mornings paper?

2. Choose from Europe at its best.

3. The new principal is the students, the parents, the teachers, and the peoples choice.

4. Mark Twains San Francisco is as vivid as Dickens London.

5. Ulysses dog recognized its master after twenty years absence.

6. A sale of ladies nylon stockings is advertised in todays paper.

7. Its also possible to get excellent values in boys and mens clothes.

8. He is always poking his nose into other peoples affairs, sometimes even into ours.

9. I don't like that particular boys manners or theirs.

10. The double consonants in *embarrassment* make its spelling a problem.

In the elevator of a hospital in Mount Vernon, N. Y., I found this sign posted:

> Childrens' Floor
> No one will be allowed on the childrens' floor without a visitors pass.

I'm sure you can do better. Print a correct sign.

### CAUTION

In your enthusiasm for apostrophes, DON'T begin putting them before the *s* in plurals. For example, the plural of *nation* is *nations;* the plural of country is *countries.*

## FINE POINT

### Use of the Possessive with Gerunds

A gerund is a participle used as a noun (e.g., *taking, having been taken*), as in all the examples that follow.

In a sentence like *I was surprised at (his, him) behaving that way,* our ear—if it's a discriminating one—leans toward *at his behaving that way,* which is equivalent to *at his behavior.* In the sentence *I was puzzled at (England's, England) reacting to the news the way she did,* the ear, I think, is more willing to accept *England.*

At any rate usage is divided—divided, it seems to me, by the Atlantic Ocean. Whereas, generally, American writers go along with the possessive form, especially with pronouns, many modern British writers seem happy with the objective case of the pronoun and the noun. I have a number of such examples from Lawrence and Gerald Durrell, C. P. Snow, E. M. Forster, F. V. Lucas, Kingsley Amis, and Brian Glanville.

Here they are. Test each sentence with your ear. If your ear likes it not, use the possessive.

1. This must prevent *him* achieving stature as an artist. (B. Glanville)

2. I remember *you* once quoting to me a passage . . . from Paracelsus. (L. Durrell)

3. I expect you remember *me* giving you occasional warnings. (C. P. Snow)

4. But he resented *him* making up to this particular woman, whom he still regarded as his enemy. (E. M. Forster)

5. Her spectacles caught the light and prevented *him* seeing where she was looking. (K. Amis)

6. We can only demand that characters shall not be so eccentric as to prevent *us* believing or feeling with them. (F. V. Lucas)

7. I peered upwards, but a slight bend in the trunk [of the tree] prevented *me* seeing very far. (G. Durrell)

Chapter 5

# Time Has More Than Three Dimensions

> I lived like the Puri Indians of whom it is said that "for yesterday, today, and tomorrow they have only one word, and they express the variety of meaning by pointing backward for yesterday, forward for tomorrow, and overhead for the passing day."
>
> —*Walden* by HENRY DAVID THOREAU

1. In which did the sharks have a feast right on the beach?
   *a.* When the old fisherman in Hemingway's *The Old Man and the Sea* got to shore, the marlin had been completely devoured by sharks.
   *b.* When the old fisherman in Hemingway's *The Old Man and the Sea* got to shore, the marlin was completely devoured by sharks.

2. Which is the more horrifying idea?
   *a.* Students at Kensington High School were given preventive medicine in case any of them came in contact with the dead boy.
   *b.* Students at Kensington High School were given preventive medicine in case any of them had come in contact with the dead boy.

3. In what kind of institution might the following conversation take place between two of the inmates? Assuming that each of the terms is the same, which one will soon be free?
   *a.* I'm here for five years.
   *b.* I've been here for five years.

4. In which case was Joe hiding?
   *a.* When Joe got home, his mother asked him where he had been.
   *b.* When Joe got home, his mother asked him where he was.

We all know that there are three kinds of time. We talk of the present, the past, and the future. There are three simple uses of the verb that correspond roughly to these three kinds of time.*

But time as measured by verbs has more than these three dimensions. For instance, here are two simple statements:

> I moved to Washington four years ago. (*moved*—past tense)
> I live in Washington now. (*live*—present tense)

Suppose we should want to combine these two ideas into one sentence, using only one verb, not two (*moved* and *live*), how could we say it?

What about, "I *have lived* in Washington for four years"? That will do it. It means exactly what we want to say. It tells of an action begun in the past (four years ago) and continuing into the present. But notice that it is neither past nor present. It is a time with a new dimension. It's another tense called the *present perfect.*

Let us examine several examples:

> Joe was a dentist for ten years.
> Joe has been a dentist for ten years.

These two statements, which look so much alike, are actually contradictory on one point. The first tells us that Joe has discontinued his practice of dentistry. The second tells us that he is still a dentist.

---

* The Chinese order these things better: One form—one—serves *all* purposes. Let's take the verb *go.* And you can stop right there! That's all there is. Then how is time shown? Easy!

*Yesterday he go. Today he go. Tomorrow he go.*

People who ignore this tense say:

1. I am a dentist for ten years.
2. Did the bell ring yet?

The first sentence tells of an action begun in the past. We should not, therefore, use *am,* a present tense. We should say *have been.* In the second sentence *yet* is an adverb meaning *up to now.* And so the present perfect, *has rung,* shows better timing—grammatically, though rarely recognized nowadays.

The present perfect tense has another use, too. It may tell of something completed at some recent *indefinite* time.

I have finished reading the book.

Whenever the past time is definitely indicated, however, the past tense must be used.

I have finished reading the book yesterday. (Correct: *finished,* past tense)*

I did it already. (Better: *I have already done it,* since the time is indefinite.)

## NOW TRY THESE

Which verb is correct?

1. I (went *or* have gone) to the circus yesterday.

2. I (didn't get *or* haven't got) my check yet.

3. I (know *or* have known) him for more than twenty years.

4. I (already did *or* have already done) it.

* Europeans are likely to make the mistake of using our present perfect tense for a *definite* past action (*I have visited the Van Gogh exhibit last night*) because in their own language the conversational past tense is made up like our present perfect—the verb *has* or *have* (sometimes *is* or *are*) plus the past participle.

5. I (am working *or* have been working) here a month.

6. He (is *or* has been) in this country only two years.

7. My brother (is *or* has been) a doctor for ten years.

8. I (made *or* have made) that point when I said I was opposed to the bill.

9. I (have *or* have had) an account in that bank for the past twenty years.

10. Joe (lived *or* has lived) on this street for four years. (Meaning that Joe no longer lives there)

## REMEMBER

The *past tense—I was there yesterday*—is used for actions entirely in the past or performed at some *definite* time in the past.

The *present perfect—I have already been there*—is used for actions begun in the past which continue through the present, or for actions performed in the *recent, indefinite* past.*

### A

For each verb in parentheses, use the tense (present, past, or present perfect) that is demanded by the meaning of the sentence.

1. There (be) fifteen members in our club now. Yesterday we (celebrate) our third anniversary. We (hold) meetings every Friday. Last year we (hold) no meetings during the summer vacation. Our club (be) in existence for three years.

* A chart of verb forms that are sometimes troublesome can be found on pages 57–59.

2. I (be) never to see a Shakespearean play, and I (be) really ashamed of myself. My friend Charles, who (see) *Othello* a week ago, (stop) not talking about how much he (enjoy) it. Therefore I (make) up my mind to see the play as soon as I can get tickets for it.

## THE PAST PERFECT TENSE

Let's look at this pair of sentences:

1. The main speaker left when Joe came in.
2. The main speaker had left when Joe came in.

In which sentence did Joe catch a glimpse of the speaker?

Obviously in sentence 1. In sentence 2, the verb *had left* shows that the speaker's leaving *preceded* Joe's entrance. Whenever two past actions are discussed together and one of them *precedes* the other, it is useful to have the past perfect to indicate the action that *came first.* When the conjunctions *before* or *after* are used, the relation of the two actions is sufficiently clear to make the use of the past perfect unnecessary.

Another use of the past perfect tense shows its resemblance to the present perfect. Just as the present perfect tense carries an action from the *past* up to the *present* so the past perfect tense carries an action from an earlier *past* to the *past* indicated by the other verb. The past perfect is especially needed when the adverbs *already* and *not yet* are used with the verb expressing the *earlier* past time: *When Keats was twenty-one; he had already* (or *not yet*) *written his best poetry.*

> I *felt* deeply hurt because he *had betrayed* my trust. (*Had betrayed,* the past perfect, is preferred to *betrayed,* the past tense, because the *betrayal* came some time before the hurt feeling.)

Jones *had played* fifty-nine minutes of the game, when he *was replaced* by a substitute. (*Had played* is called for here, since Jones's playing began in the past and continued to another point in the past, his replacement. The announcer at the game, for instance, would say, "A substitute is finally going in for Jones. Jones *has played* fifty-nine minutes of the game."

### PAST OR PAST PERFECT?

In the sentences that follow, use the past or past perfect tense for the verbs in parentheses. The first five are home-grown and easy.

1. I (come) into the room after he (leave).

2. When he (move) to the South, I (know) him for five years.

3. I (wait) there an hour, when he (come).

4. We already (decide) when you (ask) us.

5. I never (fail) before last term.

6. The spokesman (say) yesterday that a number of American combat units (serve) in the Con Thien area.

7. The general (explain) in an interview why he (reject) proposals aimed at relaxing the Spartan atmosphere in the Marine Corps.

8. She (say) in an interview that she (want) not to stay at the Waldorf Astoria in the first place.

9. A group of 30 experts on the Soviet Union (conclude) that Khrushchev's memoirs (be) authentic and (receive) the approval of the present Soviet leadership.

10. The Defense Department (deny) today that there (be) conclusive evidence that the United States Army defoliation programs (be) catastrophic for South Vietnam.

## PRINCIPAL PARTS OF VERBS

When Dizzy Dean, one of the great pitchers of baseball, was hired as announcer for games played by the St. Louis Cardinals, he became famous all over again—this time for mutilating the English language. His specialty was finding new verb forms for well-established old forms. In his broadcasts, the pitcher always "throwed" the ball hard and the batter "swang" at it. A base runner usually "slud" into second base. When the association of Missouri teachers of English complained about what he was doing to their language, he asked, "What do they want me to say—slidded?"

No, they wanted him to use the correct forms of irregular verbs (those that do not add *ed* to form the past tense and past participle). Here is a list of such verbs. Some forms may surprise you. For example, do you say, "He has swum across the lake" or "has swam across the lake"?

You'll find the answer in its alphabetical place in the list that follows.

## VERB FORMS SOMETIMES MISUSED

Capital letters indicate forms for which incorrect substitutions are sometimes made. The most serious and most often heard are *I seen* (for *saw*) and *I done it* (for *I did it*). I have included the present participle because it is sometimes misspelled.

| PRESENT | PRESENT PARTICIPLE | PAST | PAST PARTICIPLE* |
|---|---|---|---|
| arise | arising | arose | arisen |
| beat | beating | BEAT | BEATEN |
| become | becoming | became | BECOME |
| begin | beginning | BEGAN | BEGUN |
| bid (request) | bidding | BADE | BIDDEN |
| bid (make an offer | bidding | bid | BID |
| bite | biting | bit | BITTEN |
| blow | blowing | BLEW | BLOWN |
| break | breaking | broke | BROKEN |
| bring | bringing | BROUGHT | BROUGHT |
| burst | bursting | BURST | BURST |
| catch | catching | CAUGHT | CAUGHT |
| choose | choosing | CHOSE | CHOSEN |
| come | coming | CAME (not come) | COME |
| cost | costing | COST | COST |
| deal | dealing | DEALT | DEALT |
| dive | diving | DIVED or DOVE | dived or dove |
| do | doing | DID (not done) | DONE |
| drag | dragging | DRAGGED | DRAGGED |
| dream | dreaming | dreamed or dreamt | dreamed or dreamt |
| drink | drinking | DRANK | DRUNK |
| drown | drowning | DROWNED | DROWNED |
| eat | eating | ATE | EATEN |
| fall | falling | fell | FALLEN |
| fit | fitting | fitted or fit | FITTED |
| flee | fleeing | FLED | FLED |
| fly | flying | flew | FLOWN |
| forbid | forbidding | FORBADE | FORBIDDEN |
| forsake | forsaking | FORSOOK | FORSAKEN |
| freeze | freezing | froze | FROZEN |

* Used with *has* or *have, had, will have,* etc. to form the perfect tenses and with *is, was,* etc. to form the passive.

| PRESENT | PRESENT PARTICIPLE | PAST | PAST PARTICIPLE |
|---|---|---|---|
| get | getting | got | got or gotten |
| give | giving | GAVE | GIVEN |
| grow | growing | GREW | GROWN |
| hang (a picture) | hanging | hung | hung |
| hang (a criminal) | hanging | HANGED | HANGED |
| hurt | hurting | HURT | HURT |
| know | knowing | KNEW | KNOWN |
| lay | laying | LAID | LAID |
| lead | leading | LED (not lead) | LED |
| lend | lending | LENT | LENT |
| lie (recline) | lying | LAY | LAIN |
| lie (tell a lie) | lying | LIED | lied |
| lose | losing | lost | lost |
| ride | riding | rode | RIDDEN |
| ring | ringing | rang | RUNG |
| shake | shaking | shook | SHAKEN |
| sing | singing | sang or sung | SUNG |
| sink | sinking | sank or sunk | sunk or sunken |
| slay | slaying | slew | slain |
| slide | sliding | SLID | SLID |
| speak | speaking | spoke | spoken |
| stay | staying | STAYED | STAYED |
| steal | stealing | stole | STOLEN |
| string | stringing | strung | strung |
| swell | swelling | SWELLED (not swole) | swelled or swollen |
| swim | swimming | swam | SWUM |
| swing | swinging | SWUNG | swung |
| take | taking | took | TAKEN |
| tear | tearing | tore | TORN |
| throw | throwing | THREW | THROWN |

| PAST | PRESENT PARTICIPLE | PAST | PAST PARTICIPLE |
|---|---|---|---|
| wake | waking | waked or woke | waked or woken |
| wring | wringing | WRUNG | wrung |
| write | writing | wrote | written |
| win | winning | WON | WON |

## PRINCIPAL PARTS

Write the form of the past tense for each of the following verbs. Watch your spelling.

*Example:* steal *Answer:* stole

| | |
|---|---|
| 1. do | 11. bring |
| 2. come | 12. seek |
| 3. lead | 13. choose |
| 4. lie (to rest) | 14. run |
| 5. lie (to tell an untruth) | 15. win |
| 6. lay | 16. grow |
| 7. see | 17. drink |
| 8. pay | 18. flee |
| 9. ring | 19. give |
| 10. beat | 20. slay |

In each of the following sentences, select the correct form of the verb:

1. After the game he (drank, drunk) a whole quart of water.
2. I (saw, seen) him do it with my own eyes.
3. He (did, done) it again last week.
4. Yesterday he (came, come) in late again.
5. Prices have always (rose, risen) during a war period.

6. I have (gone, went) home early all this week.

7. He has (ran, run) all the way to tell us the news.

8. The ball is (lieing, lying) where you (threw, throwed) it.

9. Who has (taken, took) my pen?

10. He has (swam, swum) across the lake several times.

11. I (beat, bet) him 21 to 15 in the Ping-Pong finals.

12. He (lead, led) the procession down the street.

## FINE POINTS: THE SUBJUNCTIVE

Although the subjunctive is alive and well and living in France, Spain, Italy, and Germany, it is virtually—with few exceptions—dead in England* and America.

Most of us quite naturally say, "If I *were* you," without realizing that *I were* is not normally a grammatical sequence. This is the subjunctive, contrary to fact. *If I were you* says *I am not you.* This use is confined largely to *I*. One finds *If he was here now* (he *isn't*) perhaps more often than *If he were here* in the writings of modern authors.

Perhaps you have noticed another peculiarity: *were,* in *If I were there* (I *am* not there), is equivalent to the present tense.

Do we have a past tense? Yes, and we use it quite naturally without realizing that we are handling something as formidable as the subjunctive. We say, *If he had been here yesterday* (he *wasn't*), *all the trouble would have been avoided.* What looks like a past perfect tense *(he had been)* is the past subjunctive contrary to fact.

* Not quite dead. In a book published in 1970 by a distinguished British writer, I found this sentence: "Both believed that every work of art, whether it were a house, a garden, or a poem, should be a judicious blend of art and nature."

In the use of this *had* form we must be careful of two things:

1. We should not use the ordinary past: *If he was* (or *were*) *here yesterday, all the trouble would have been avoided.*

2. We should avoid using *would have* in both halves, even if some writers occasionally do so. For example, *If he would have been there, all the trouble would have been avoided.*

Why? Let's just say that the word *would* has a future idea in it and the tense is obviously past. But you may want to ask, "What about the second part: *the trouble would have been avoided?* Isn't that future too?" Yes, it is; it is future to the first *have. If this had been done, this would have happened.* If all this puzzles you, forget it. Just avoid it and let it go at that.

Sometimes the subjunctive is used to indicate a future possibility, as in *If I were to ask you for help,* etc. *If I were to live in a wilderness,* etc.

## EXERCISE IN SUBJUNCTIVES

Remembering that *were* is to *would* as *had been* is to *would have,* try yourself out on the following. You can even say of some sentences that either *was* or *were* is acceptable. Certainly, where *if* equals *whether, was* (not *were*) should be used. Some sentences may be correct as they are.

1. Experts agree that if it weren't for the Nixon vote, the district would have sent a Democrat to Congress.

2. "If I was the Mayor, I'd sit this one out," the Governor commented.

3. "If you would have known of this," the judge said, "you would have realized he was a not-so-innocent little schoolboy with a bow tie."

4. For a moment I wondered if she was going to cry.

5. If anyone said that fifty years ago, he would have been considered mad.

6. He was asked if it were the usual custom in Mississippi in primary contests to have a rerun of the two top candidates.

7. Let the court take note of the fact that if I were permitted to leave the country, there would have been no criminal plot.

8. One highly placed Turkish official warned that Turkey was quite willing to fight if she were invaded.

9. Anne would have been particularly obliged to her cousin if he would have walked by her side without saying a word.

10. If I knew all the facts, I wouldn't have acted so hastily.

### Good Advice

The subjunctive in English is on the way out. Say or write what comes naturally. You'll probably do as well as most writers.

## YOU CAN RELAX

Once upon a time a good deal of fuss was made about whether to use *shall* or *will*. It was even necessary to anticipate the reply and ask, "Shall you be at the theater tonight?" because the expected answer would be, "I shall (or shall not)."

Today *will* is the verb permissible in all cases except when a threat, warning, or prohibition is expressed. For example, "The demonstration *shall* not take place on the Capitol steps" means that the protesters are warned against using the Capitol steps for their demonstration. (*Will* in this sentence would mean that the demonstrators do not plan to use the Capitol steps.)

Note that most of the Commandments begin with: "Thou shalt not." *Thou shalt not kill* is a prohibition. *Thou wilt not kill* is an expression of faith and hope.

You can relax even more with *should* and *would*. The use of *I should like* or *I should prefer* is rarely heard. Not one person in a hundred knows what the difference between *should* and *would* is and not one in a thousand cares.

## THE SO-CALLED SPLIT INFINITIVE

There are some who still worry about splitting an infinitive down the middle by inserting an adverb between the *to* and the verb form. You can relax here, too. Is there a better place for *really* in: *To* really *understand* this problem, etc. or for *steadily* in: *To steadily increase* Canada's foreign aid contributions, etc.

Jimmy Durante once said: "When I goes to work on an infinitive I don't just split it; I break it in little pieces."

Don't go too far in splitting infinitives by writing a sentence such as: I'm going *to* as a favor to you even though you didn't ask me for it *arrange* all the details for your climb up Mt. Rainier.

That's no split; that's a crevasse.

Chapter 6

# If You Speak English Good, You Don't Speak It Well: Adjectives and Adverbs

A THIEF'S GRAMMAR CATCHES UP TO HIM

Polson, Montana (AP)—It is bad enough to split an infinitive but if you misspell an adverb you could be left dangling from your own participle.

One piece of evidence in the case was a note taken from the safe in the business office. The locked safe bore this notice:

"This safe contains papers only
for protection from fire."

Above the typed statement, the burglar had scribbled: "I read and I'll leave it He Ha," plus an afterthought that proved his undoing: "To cops went pass me."

The suspect in the case was asked to write the same sentence and he repeated exactly the misspelled words, confusing adjectives with infinitives and adverbs with verbs.

—From AP dispatch.

Now that you know some grammar, you know that the burglar in the AP dispatch obviously doesn't. He has confused prepositional phrases with infinitives and nouns with prepositions.

"To cops" is *not* an infinitive. It is made up of a preposition *to* and a noun *cops* which would make it a prepositional phrase. What is needed is *two,* of course, an adjective to modify the noun *cops.*

"Pass" all by itself may be either a verb or a noun, not an adverb. What is needed here is *past,* a preposition, with the object *me.*

Now that we have disposed of the burglar's grammatical knowledge, try yours on the following sentences concerned chiefly with adjectives or adverbs.

1. Who will be able to claim a deduction for charitable contributions?
   *a.* He's done good with the money he inherited.
   *b.* He's done well with the money he inherited.

2. Which statement has a sock in it?
   *a.* It's darned good.
   *b.* It's darned well.

3. Which dog is definitely not a bloodhound?
   *a.* The dog smells bad.
   *b.* The dog smells badly.

4. Which one is more to be feared?
   *a.* He's the kind of fellow who takes life easy.
   *b.* He's the kind of fellow who takes life easily.

5. Which assures you of an easy climb?
   *a.* You will find the mountain trail easy.
   *b.* You will find the mountain trail easily.

6. In which sentence is Joe being sized up?
   *a.* Joe looked careful.
   *b.* Joe looked carefully.

## PRETEST

1. I can't stand a person who speaks (indistinct, indistinctly).

2. I like a person who dresses (simple, simply), not (flashy, flashily).

3. She looks (beautiful, beautifully) in her new outfit.

4. After taking several lessons from the pro he hit the ball (different, differently).

5. The soft ice cream tastes (delicious, deliciously).

6. She played the Chopin études (beautiful, beautifully).

7. To avoid accidents, drive (careful, carefully).

8. She ran as (graceful, gracefully) as a gazelle.

9. He was (near, nearly) dead when they found him.

10. He got along very (good, well) in mathematics but very (bad, badly) in English.

11. You've done very (good, well) so far; let's try one more.

12. Nick isn't doing so (bad, badly) with a tail-end club.

## ADJECTIVE OR ADVERB?

As you have already seen, an adjective modifies a noun, generally answering the question, "What kind of?" (e.g., in a *courteous* manner, *courteous* answers the question "What kind of?")

An adverb modifies a verb, an adjective, or another adverb and answers questions such as "Why?" "How?" "When?" "How much?"

## GOOD OR WELL?

*Good* is an adjective. The adverbial equivalent of *good* is *well.* However, the American people, listening to radio or watching television, reading advertisements or the comics, are being sold the use of *good* as an adverb.

Practically every MC on a game program gets off a remark like, "You've done very *good* so far." TV commercials ask watchers to "rub it in *good*" or "soak it *good*." Listeners to a play-by-play report of a baseball game hear: "His sinker is working *good* today" or "He certainly hit the ball *good* but right into the hands of Willie Mays." A newspaper advertisement asks the reader to LISTEN GOOD.

Nevertheless and despite all this, the word to use in all these instances is *well*—if you want to master *good* English and speak it *well*. (The Usage Panel voted almost unanimously against the use of good for *well* in written English, while 73 percent found *good* for *well* unacceptable in spoken English.)

However, *good* can and should be used after verbs that are like the verb *to be* (e.g., *to seem, to appear*) and when verbs like *look, smell, taste, feel,* etc. are passive in meaning.

For example: Does she look *beautiful* or *beautifully* in her new outfit?

The answer, of course, is *beautiful*. She isn't *looking* (an active verb); she is *being looked at* (a passive verb).

But the verb look can also show action: She *looked carefully* at the pictures to be sure to select the best one. Now *she* is looking and we need an adverb to tell the *how* of the action.

Let's look at a few more.

> The apple tastes (sweet or sweetly).
> The fish smells (fresh or freshly).
> The cool air feels (good or well).

You can see that in each of these sentences *tastes, smells,* and *feels* can be equated with *is;* hence, the adjective follows, not the adverb.

I might add here that for years a controversy has been raging over whether to say, "I felt bad or I felt badly about the tragic situation." Grammatically, *bad* is correct but somehow inadequate. *Bad* seems a weak word for an emotion that may be very strong. Therefore, some prefer *badly* in this case. Editorials have been written in newspapers on this particular dilemma with no decision reached. Let your decision rest with the intensity of the feeling.

There's no such difficulty with *good.* I felt *good* or *happy* or *anxious* or *euphoric.*

## EXERCISE CHIEFLY ON GOOD AND WELL

1. He ran into hard luck just as he seemed to be getting along (good, well) on a 2 to 1 lead in the fourth.

2. Can we force him to do it (different, differently)?

3. The flower smells (sweet, sweetly).

4. Some people take things like that very (serious, seriously).

5. Let's see how (good, well) we can do in this round.

6. There was no structural damage from the earthquake but things rattled around pretty (good, well).

7. If I had hit (good, well) I'd still be there, but each year you don't play (regular, regularly), the worse you get.

8. I wish I could sing as (good, well) as Rex Harrison did in *My Fair Lady.*

9. I have never won anything playing too (cautious, cautiously).

10. You have to feel (confident, confidently) and take a big cut at the ball.

11. When he explained the details to me I felt (different, differently) about the whole situation.

12. Congratulations, Andy! You played (marvelous, marvelously) today.

13. The contents of the bulging can of soup smelled (strange, strangely)

14. Whenever I see a sad picture like *Love Story,* I feel (bad, badly) for hours afterward.

15. A rose by any other name would smell as (sweet, sweetly).

## ADJECTIVES IN LY

Although we usually distinguish between the adjective and the adverb form by the ending *ly,* there are a number of adjectives that end in *ly:*

> cowardly, daily, motherly, early, friendly, leisurely, lively, lovely, orderly, etc.

Some of these may be used conveniently as adverbs:

> The paper was delivered *daily.*

It is inadvisable, however, to use most of the others as anything but adjectives. The following sound pretty bad (not *badly*):

> She treated me motherly.
> They marched out of the theater orderly.
> He greeted me very friendly.

In such cases you generally do better if you use a phrase instead:

> She treated me like a mother.
> They marched out of the theater in an orderly manner.
> He greeted me in a very friendly way.

## ADVERBS WITHOUT LY

There are a number of short adjectives which may under certain conditions properly and effectively be used as adverbs even when there is a corresponding adverb ending in *ly* (e.g., traffic sign: GO SLOW; but *he went slowly about his business*). A partial list would include, besides *slow,* such words as *close, deep, direct, fair, fine, hard, high, loud, low, quick, right, straight, tight, wrong.**

Those who are too cautious often add *ly* unnecessarily to some of these words and get ineffective or curious results.

*He did fine* is certainly better than *finely, finely* being reserved for such phrases as *finely strung, finely knit.*

In the sentence, *In this North Sea village you can buy your fish direct from the fisherman at his hut,* the word *direct* is to be preferred to *directly.* And surely no one says *He hit the ball hardly.* Don't be timid; depending on the meaning, it is all right to use these words with verbs and without *ly* endings. Your ear will often be a reliable guide.

## THEY COME IN SIZES TOO

Under the state marketing agreement in California, olives are graded according to these size standards:

> medium, large, larger, mammoth, giant, jumbo, colossal, and supercolossal

thus making *large* olives almost the *smallest* obtainable.

---

* It is obvious that in certain meanings the *ly* word is the only one to use. *He kicked the ball deep into enemy territory* but *He hurt me deeply. Play fair* but *He was beaten fairly.* Note that if we add an *ly* to *low* (which can be used as either an adjective or adverb) it becomes *lowly* (adjective only).

Grammatically, however, there are only three sizes:

| POSITIVE | COMPARATIVE | SUPERLATIVE |
|---|---|---|
| large | larger | largest |
| small | smaller | smallest |

H*y*m*a*n K*a*p*l*a*n once startled his night school teacher with:

| | | |
|---|---|---|
| bad | worse | *rotten* |
| good | better | *high-class* |
| cold | colder | *below zero* |

instead of the more orthodox *worst, best,* and *coldest.*

When Shakespeare has Marc Antony say, "This was the most unkindest cut of all," we admire the intensity of feeling Shakespeare achieved by being ungrammatical. However, when *you* do something like that don't expect congratulations.

Omit *more* or *most* if the meaning remains unchanged.

1. He was a more gentler person than people thought.

2. Because of his great wealth he felt more superior.

3. This was the most costliest day for our helicopter squadron.

4. Confidentially, I think Conrad's plans more preferable.

5. He is a lot more friendlier than his brother.

6. It is a beautiful day but the proclamation of peace has made it that much more brighter.

Note that the following is correct: "More colder weather is expected for tomorrow."

## FINE POINTS

### Quantitatively Speaking

Don't settle for *less* where the sense calls for *fewer*, and it calls for *fewer* if the noun following is in the plural (e.g., *less bread, fewer rolls; less time, fewer days*).

When Pamela Hansford Johnson (Mrs. C. P. Snow) in *The New York Times Book Review* wrote: "We English use less prepositions than you do," she and *The Times* received hundreds of letters protesting the use of *less* for *fewer*. She graciously wrote to the editor: "First, admission and apologies. No, 'less prepositions' isn't very nice; I agree. My acknowledgments to all grammarians who have written privately and publicly."

When considering words of quantity, here's an easy rule.

> little money—few dollars
>
> much money—many dollars
>
> less money—fewer dollars

Where a *unit* of time or money is involved *less* may be used.

> He had *less* than ten dollars with him.
> He had served *less* than three years.

BUT

> *Fewer* troops in Southeast Asia means *less* money spent on the military.

The only other adjectives that give this kind of trouble are *this* and *that* (plural *these* and *those*) and they give trouble only when used with the words *kind, sort,* and *type*. We are tempted to say *these kind of books* and *those kind of remarks.* However, since *kind, sort,* and *type* are *singular,* they should be preceded by *this* or *that.*

When a statesman recently scouted "those sorts of rumors," he was being grammatically accurate. To many of us, however, "those sorts of rumors" and "that sort of rumors" seem stilted. Fortunately, we have our choice of the following correct substitutes:

> that sort of rumor (correct)
> rumors of that sort (correct)

*Almost* means *very nearly; most* means the greater or greatest number. Except in informal speech it is inadvisable to use *most* in sentences like:

*Most everybody makes some kind of mistake in English usage.* (Preferred: *almost;* 92 percent of the Usage Panel found it unacceptable in formal writing, but divided almost evenly on its use in informal speech.)

*Most* can, of course, be correctly used to mean *very,* as in *I was most pleased by the attention he gave me.* (But even this can get you into trouble, as it did one young man who, shaking hands with the new minister on the church steps, said, "And I suppose that this is your most beautiful wife?" "My only one," replied the minister.)

## EXERCISE ON USE OF LESS AND FEWER, MOST AND ALMOST

1. Is it true, I'd like to know, that (less, fewer) accidents occur on our highways than in our homes?

2. Her articles in a variety of magazines appear in (almost, most) all of the national magazines.

3. Stonewall Jackson once sent the following terse telegram to the War Department at Richmond: "Send me more men and (less, fewer) questions."

4. In France alone it sold 840,000 copies in hardcover and almost as (much, many) in paperback.

5. In the twinkling of an eye and long before the white pellet vanished (deep, deeply) into the lower right-field stand (most, almost) everyone in the ballpark knew it was all over.

6. The test results also brought out that in the elementary grades there were (less, fewer) pupils below the norm than a year ago.

7. It was a rare exhibition between two hurlers who had (most, almost) everything.

8. We then had 228 (less, fewer) ships than we have now.

9. You would find him (almost, most) every morning at his easel in the studio.

10. There are now only 300,000 (less, fewer) smoking women than in 1966 despite a population increase of three million adult women.

## A FEW ODD ONES

Such words as *perfect, correct, round,* and *unique* seem in their original form to express a superlative, and we are often warned never to use them with *more* or *most.*

Yet Samuel Johnson, in the introduction to his famous dictionary, says, "The words here are *more correctly* spelled."

And our own Constitution has in its first sentence the thrilling phrase, "In order to form a *more perfect* union."

We probably feel that nothing is really perfect, eternally correct, or absolutely round.

Those who worry about this sort of thing can, if they wish, say *more nearly round, more nearly correct,* and *more nearly perfect,* while the rest of us go right on upholding the Constitution.

*Unique,* however, which means *the only one* of its kind, is unique and nothing can be *more unique.*

## OTHER

Use *other* when comparing things or persons of the same kind or class.

*Correct:* The pitcher works harder than any *other* player on the team.

To be strictly logical, we should use *other* since the pitcher is included in *any player on the team* and cannot work harder than himself.

But leave out *other* when the two things compared are in different classifications.

*Correct:* An elephant can run faster than any human being.

## DUE TO

Ordinarily the word *due* is an adjective (adverb—*duly*) in such sentences as *The due date for the manuscript was June 1, 1971,* or *The rent is due.*

Strictly construed, therefore, the phrase *due to* should be used only where an adjective modifier is called for, as in the following:

> Lateness, due to traffic snarls, is not unusual.
> His lateness was due to a traffic snarl.

In spite of the frequent use in writing of *due to* in an adverbial position to show causal relation, 84 percent of the Usage Panel find it unacceptable—even in the face of such a fixed expression as *Due to circumstances beyond his control.**

* If I were a betting man, I'd wager that 99 out of 100 business letters of a certain kind begin with: "Due to increased overhead, new equipment, and maintenance costs, we have found it necessary. . . ."

What shall we use instead?

> Due to the muddy roads, the tank offensive was bogged down. (Strictly: *because of* or *on account of*)

CHANGE THESE IF YOU WANT TO

1. Due to the bad weather, the game between the Mets and Dodgers was called off.

2. Due in part to the momentum which the President and his aides generated, Congress last year established five new national parks.

3. Due to a taxi accident, her right hand was so badly injured that it is doubtful whether she will ever be able to play the piano again.

## Chapter 7

# Can You Save a Dangling Modifier or Participle?

A 'LESSON' IN ENGLISH

And an Army Trainee Learns About 'the Misplaced Modifier'

Pullman, Washington (AP)—An army trainee in a Washington State College classroom asked this question:

"Sir, can you tell us whether we have to take this English class during the whole gol-dinged nine months we're here?"

Prof. Lewis E. Buchanan replied:

"Gentlemen, there you see a perfect example of the misplaced modifier. Obviously what this gentleman means is, 'Do you have to take this gol-dinged English class the whole nine months you are here?' "

—From AP dispatch, September, 1970

1. To which question, asked by David Susskind of a panel of photographers, was one of them justified in answering, "She's a lousy photographer"?

   *a.* What do you think of Ingrid Bergman as a photographer?

   *b.* As a photographer, what do you think of Ingrid Bergman?

2. In which sentence was the baseball battered?

   *a.* In the second inning the pitcher sustained a gash on the chin from a batted ball that required six stitches.

   *b.* In the second inning a batted ball hit the pitcher's chin, making a gash that required six stitches.

3. Which persons valued their lives cheaply?
   *a.* The obituary column lists the names of persons who died recently for a nominal fee.
   *b.* The obituary column for a nominal fee lists the names of persons who died recently.

4. Which is unfair to the local fire department?
   *a.* The blaze was put out before any damage was done by the local fire department.
   *b.* The blaze was put out by the local fire department before any damage was done.

5. Which arrangement would be a bother for the First Lady?
   *a.* Our guests are then taken to the famous Hotel Willow within walking distance of the White House, where rooms are provided for them.
   *b.* Our guests are then taken to their rooms at the famous Hotel Willow within walking distance of the White House.

6. In which statement is the Argentinian President accused of being a troublemaker?
   *a.* Whether the Argentinian Communists deliberately chose to cause trouble during a period when they knew their President was going to the United States, or whether the course of events rose to a natural climax is hard to tell.
   *b.* Whether the Argentinian Communists deliberately chose a period when they knew their President was going to the United States to cause trouble, or whether the course of events rose to a natural climax is hard to tell.

7. Which statement is incredible on the face of it?
   *a.* Although a Protestant, the Pope received me most graciously.
   *b.* Although I am a Protestant, the Pope received me most graciously.

It is always best to have a phrase modifier as near as possible to the word it belongs with. If these modifiers are placed somewhere else, you may come up with a sentence like this (one newspaper did):

> The Dodger outfielder is still raging over the report that he slugged a photographer carried in an afternoon paper.

As you can see, that is rather an uncomfortable position for a photographer to be in. It was the report, of course, that was carried in an afternoon paper. What to do? Put "carried in an afternoon paper" where it belongs.

> The Dodger outfielder is still raging over the report, carried in an afternoon paper, that he slugged a photographer.

On the jacket of *The Annotated Walden* (edited by Philip Van Doren Stern) appears this sentence:

> Henry David Thoreau lived from July 4, 1845, to September 6, 1847, in the cabin he had built on the shores of Walden Pond.

How much better this sentence would be if we were to put *from July 4, 1845, to September 6, 1847,* at the beginning. This is often a good way of dealing with a stranded phrase. It results in a sentence that ends with a bang instead of a whimper. (See first sentence below.)

## TEST ON MISPLACED MODIFIERS

(The first eight are taken from newspaper stories or advertisements. Sometimes a remark is added to help you locate the trouble.)

1. He was born the year after President Lincoln's assassination at Florence, a farm town in northwestern Alabama. (And we always thought Ford's Theater was in Washington.)

2. Be sure to purchase enough yarn to finish your article before you start. (Even a computer couldn't do that.)

3. You get more U.S. prime quality because our meats are selected by our perfectionist butchers, aged at least three weeks. (Not child labor again!)

4. We recommend *The Heiress,* a gripping story of a woman's vengeance on the CBS television network. (Still another attack on the media?)

5. You can order a dress that will be delivered to you by telephone. (To the wrong number?)

6. Herman Melville had to seek the companionship and understanding he never received from his mother and father in other people.

7. The whole family complimented Susan on the fine performance she gave as they were leaving the auditorium. (Free open-air concert?)

8. Israel has developed a bulletproof helmet for soldiers made of plastic. (What will they think of next?)

9. Ellen sat watching the gull fly back and forth over the dunes in a red bathing suit. (Showing off!)

10. The best fruit he likes is peaches. (Don't people always like the best?)

## PARTICIPLES ARE SOMETIMES LEFT UP IN THE AIR

> One couldn't help but be aware of the stallion Royal Rick sitting in the stands the last couple of nights of the spring meeting at Toronto Greenwood.
>
> —From Guelph (Ont.) Standardbred Record

Showing how a racehorse can be made into an interested spectator.

1. Which judge seems also to be a philanthropist?
   *a.* Having paid my parking fine, I was dismissed by the judge with a reprimand.

*b.* Having paid my parking fine, the judge dismissed me with a reprimand.

2. Which bus belongs in Disneyland?
   *a.* Hopping from one tired foot to the other, the crosstown bus finally came into view.
   *b.* Hopping from one tired foot to the other, I finally saw the crosstown bus come into view.

3. Which boys should be studying Latin or Greek instead of bucking the line?
   *a.* Being of fragile material, the boys on the football team are having a hard time keeping their jerseys intact.
   *b.* Being of fragile material, the jerseys worn by the boys on the football team are hard to keep intact.

4. Which case should be reported to the American Society for the Prevention of Cruelty to Animals?
   *a.* Having broken both its front legs, they carried the dog to the veterinarian.
   *b.* Having broken both its front legs, the dog was carried to the veterinarian.

5. In which case have students' rights gone a bit too far?
   *a.* After taking a test, the faculty panel accepted me as a candidate for a degree.
   *b.* After taking a test, I was accepted by the panel as a candidate for a degree.

A participle usually performs the function of an adjective, which gives us information about a noun or pronoun. You must, therefore, be sure that it is hanging on to a noun or pronoun which makes the sense you intend.

The sentence, *Walking across the street, a truck almost ran me down,* is absurd. Obviously the truck was not walking; I was. Therefore the sentence should read *Walking across the street, I was almost run down by a truck.* Or we can get rid of the participle and write: *As I walked across the street, a truck almost ran me down.*

In the paired sentences you have just completed, each

of the sentences is correct but the meanings are far apart, and one suspects that one of the meanings was not intended by the writer.

Make each of the following sentences clearer by giving the participial phrase something to hang on to by changing it to a dependent clause. The first six sentences appeared in print as they appear here:

1. When caught, the hunting knife was still in the subject's hand, the police said.

2. Having fought in World War II, your August 21 editorial "Civilian Casualties in Vietnam" is puzzling.

3. Sold to the public like a packet of soap powder, the voters have bought the candidate just before the holes begin to show in their washing.

4. When visiting Russia, the everyday household chores may seem very unusual to an American but not to a European.

5. Convinced that widespread reading of this article will help curb reckless driving, reprints in leaflet form are offered at cost.

6. Though beginning to fade, I think St. Louis will furnish the closest competition.

7. After being dead for more than 150 years, Beethoven's music is still loved by many people.

8. Upon entering the plane, the stewardess gave me a stick of chewing gum.

9. Walking in from the darkness, a dazzling white, lifelike statue of Lincoln greets you.

10. Walking along the edge of the lake, a fish suddenly jumped out of the water.

Chapter 8

# Don't Confuse Them or Misuse Them

> Once I remember I used the words *sarcasm* and *irony* in an English essay. Mr. H. read them out and asked me what I meant by them and told the class he bet I didn't know. I replied that sarcasm was making fun of people, as he was making fun of me, but that irony was when the truth was funny.
>
> —From *The Golden Echo* by DAVID GARNETT

A study of the paired sentences that follow shows how the mere interchange of words may result in a complete change in meaning.

## WORDS CONFUSED OR MISUSED

1. Which Joe resembles the great Sherlock Holmes?
   *a.* Joe deducted it from the other items presented to him.
   *b.* Joe deduced it from the other items presented to him.

2. In which sentence did the first-nighters miss a speech about the weather?
   *a.* On the opening night a gun refused to fire and a premature curtain cut off a climatic speech.
   *b.* On the opening night a gun refused to fire and a premature curtain cut off a climactic speech.

3. In which production did the actors look like giants?
   *a.* In the production of *Our Town* no scenery was used and very little props.
   *b.* In the production of *Our Town* no scenery was used and very few props.

4. Which performance made Iago seem real?
   *a.* His performance in the controversial role of Iago was credible.
   *b.* His performance in the controversial role of Iago was creditable.

5. Which theater had only six people in the audience?
   *a.* In the audience there were five people beside me.
   *b.* In the audience there were five people besides me.

6. Which is the better deal for the professional boxers?
   *a.* Both heavyweights will get $2,500,000.
   *b.* Each heavyweight will get $2,500,000.

7. Which is by way of being an ultimatum?
   *a.* I'll give you an instant to prove it.
   *b.* I'll give you an instance to prove it.

8. Which was more like a vacation?
   *a.* Joe stood in the country for two weeks.
   *b.* Joe stayed in the country for two weeks.

9. Which would Joe's mother prefer?
   *a.* Joe took the dirty stray dog home.
   *b.* Joe brought the dirty stray dog home.

10. Which was the more complete job?
   *a.* The bandits robbed the truck.
   *b.* The bandits stole the truck.

11. In which case was Joe cashing in on his father's prominence?
   *a.* Joe flouted his father's authority.
   *b.* Joe flaunted his father's authority.

12. Which is an act of generosity?
   *a.* He went to the library to lend a rare book.
   *b.* He went to the library to borrow a rare book.

13. Which judge would most lawyers prefer?
    *a.* The judge was completely disinterested.
    *b.* The judge was completely uninterested.

14. Which required more ingenuity?
    *a.* He adopted his sister's plan.
    *b.* He adapted his sister's plan.

15. Which does not violate the principle of freedom of speech?
    *a.* The Commission's report was censored by the President.
    *b.* The Commission's report was censured by the President.

16. In which case did the protesters futilely use feathers?
    *a.* The protesters laid down on the highway to hold up traffic.
    *b.* The protesters lay down on the highway to hold up traffic.

17. Which sentence means, "Don't include me"?
    *a.* Leave me out.
    *b.* Let me out.

18. Which shouldn't be said even to a dog?
    *a.* Lie down, Fido.
    *b.* Lay down Fido.

19. In which case is an accusing finger being pointed?
    *a.* The newspaper lay right here.
    *b.* The newspaper lied right here.

20. In which case has the quality of your English improved?
    *a.* Since reading this book I make fewer serious mistakes in English.
    *b.* Since reading this book I make less serious mistakes in English.

### ACCEPT, EXCEPT

*Accept* means to take something that is offered; *except* means to leave out.

*Correct:* All those over forty-five are excepted from this ruling.
*Correct:* We accept the ruling without protest.

### ADAPT, ADOPT

When you *adopt* something you take it over as it is, lock, stock, and barrel.

When you *adapt* something you change it to suit new circumstances. You can *adopt* someone else, but you *adapt* yourself.

*Correct:* He *adopted* a little English girl.
*Correct:* Margaret tried to *adapt* herself to her new environment.

You can *adopt* or *adapt* a plan, depending on whether you take it as it is *(adopt)* or change it to suit your needs *(adapt)*.

### ADMISSION, ADMITTANCE

Often used interchangeably, except in the following instances:

Positively no admittance
The price of admission
A dangerous admission (of fact or evidence)

### AFFECT, EFFECT

*Affect,* as a verb, means to influence. *Effect,* as a verb, means to bring about as a result; as a noun it means the result or consequence.

*Correct:* His speech *affected* the audience greatly.

*Correct:* The antibiotics *effected* a remarkable cure with no noticeable side *effects.*

ALUMNA, ALUMNAE ALUMNUS, ALUMNI

On the left we have a female graduate and female graduates (pronounced *nee*); on the extreme right, male graduates (pronounced *nigh*). You can save a lot of trouble by using the word *graduate* or *graduates.*

AMBIGUOUS, EQUIVOCAL

Though generally used interchangeably to mean having two or more possible interpretations, the nice distinction made is that while *ambiguity* is always unintentional, *equivocation* may be purposeful, intending to deceive.

An ambiguous statement is made by someone who doesn't make himself clear, while an *equivocal* statement is made by someone who doesn't want to make himself clear. Anybody can be *ambiguous,* but you have to be clever to be able to *equivocate*—a diplomat, for example, an official spokesman, the Delphic Oracle, or the witches in *Macbeth,* of whom Macbeth complains that they deal with him in a "double sense: that keep the word of promise to our ear, and break it to our hope."

APT, LIKELY, LIABLE

When followed by infinitives these three words show the following differences in meaning:

*Apt* shows a strong inherent or habitual tendency. *She is apt to exaggerate.*

*Likely* tells of probability. *She is likely to arrive at any time.*

*Liable* emphasizes *only* a *bad* outcome. *It it liable to explode in your hands.*

If these words bother you, there's an easy way out. Whenever there's any doubt use *likely*. It is the most flexible of the three words and will almost always be satisfactory for any of the three meanings.

### AVENGE, REVENGE

The verb *avenge* refers to a nobler, more righteous and more altruistic action than *revenge* (verb and noun). To *revenge* is to seek retaliation for *personal* gratification.

### BET, BEAT

To *bet* means to make a wager.
To *beat* means to win from, to conquer.

### BESIDE, BESIDES

Though often interchanged, *besides* should be used when the meaning is *in addition to; beside,* for *alongside.*

*Besides me* = in addition to me
*Beside me* = next to, alongside me

### BETWEEN, AMONG

The rule, as generally stated, tells us that *between* should be used for *two* and *among* for *more than two.* We say quite properly: *He divided it between my brother and me,* or *He divided it among his four children.*

However, when *among* sounds awkward in cases where we wish to have the items considered *separately,* we use *between* for more than two.

Take, for instance, this sentence from a book review: "But he has never distinguished, as George Dangerfield said so well, 'between three quite distinct things: contemporary journalism, a sermon—and a Chill Down the Spine.' "

And I don't think we would say, "What is the difference *among* allusion, delusion, and illusion?"

But be sure when using *between* that there are two items it can be between.

*Avoid:*

One of the spectators rose to his feet between each inning. (Correct: *after each inning* or *between innings*)

We went out to the lobby between each act. (Correct: *between acts*)

BORROW, LEND, LOAN

We *borrow from;* we *lend to.*

*Avoid:*

I *lent* a nickel from him. (Correct: *borrowed*)

He *loaned* a hundred dollars from the bank. (Correct: *borrowed*)

*Lend* and *loan* are now used almost interchangeably, though *lend* is still preferred in all cases except where finances are involved.

*Avoid:*

the use of *lend* as a noun

May I have the lend of your fountain pen for a minute? (Correct: *May I borrow* or *Please lend me*)

BOTH, EACH

*Both* and *each* should not be used interchangeably. *Both* means *two together; each* means any number taken one at a time. The use of *both* for *each* results in ambiguity. When a sports reporter writes: "Yastzremski got two singles, both of them driving in two runs," we're not sure what is meant. How many runs did Yastzremski bring in? Two or four? It makes it much clearer to say:

"Yastzremski got two singles, each of which drove in two runs." Now we can add two and two and get four.

> "Do both of these picture frames cost five dollars?" "No, ma'am. Both cost ten dollars; each of them costs five." (Correct, proving that the customer is not always right)

Also notice that we don't put *the* before the word *both: Both of us,* not *the both of us.*

## BRING, TAKE

To *bring* means to carry toward the speaker or to his home (analogous to *Come here*).

To *take* means to carry away from the speaker *(Go there).*

You *bring* someone home when you are going to your own home.

You *take* someone home when you act as an escort.

But don't get uptight about these verbs, the way a friend of mine, a chemistry teacher, did a long time ago. He needed a thermos bottle for an experiment he was going to perform that week. To make sure he'd have it at school, he decided to write himself a postcard. "Dear Jess," he wrote. "Bring a thermos bottle to school on Thursday." He read over what he had written and began to frown. "Let's see. *Bring* is right because I want it here at school. But tomorrow when I get this card, I'll be at home, so it should really be *Take* a thermos bottle to school." He mumbled, "Bring, take; take, bring." Finally, he tore up the card and wrote another. All it said was, "Don't forget the thermos bottle."

CAN, MAY

*Can* means to be able to; *may* means to have permission to. The distinction has become almost completely blurred by usage.

When my little girl was in 4A she told me that whenever a pupil in her class raised his hand and asked, "Can I leave the room?" the teacher invariably replied, *"Can* you? How do I know? I don't know whether you are *able* to. But you *may."* Despite these heroic efforts, the distinction between *can* and *may,* especially in questions, is gradually disappearing.

Avoid the unnecessary use of *could* when *can* is what is meant.

> My brother is versatile; he *could* do anything.
> Anagrams is a fine game; any number *could* play.

(Isn't *can* better?)

CAPITAL, CAPITOL

Capital is the city; capitol, the building.

CENSOR, CENSURE, CRITICIZE

To *censor* is to exercise the right of deleting or forbidding; to *censure* is to scold; to *criticize* mean to evaluate favorably as well as unfavorably, though it is more frequently used to mean faultfinding.

CHILDISH, CHILDLIKE

*Childish* refers to the worst features of a child; *childlike,* to the best. If you call a girl *childish,* she won't like it; if you tell her she is *childlike,* in the right tone of voice —slightly husky and adoring—she will probably like it.

*Childish* means like a child in foolishness.

*Childlike* means like a child in features, innocence, and so on.

### CLIMATIC, CLIMACTIC

I have frequently heard and also seen in print *climatic* when *climactic* was meant. *Climactic* is the adjective form of *climax* and therefore the *c* must appear in the word and be pronounced.

*Climatic* is the adjective form of *climate* and therefore refers to weather conditions.

### COMPLEMENTARY, COMPLIMENTARY

The first serves to fill out or *complete;* the second expresses or contains a *compliment.*

The words used at the end of a letter (Yours sincerely, Cordially yours, etc.) are called the complimentary close.

### CONTEMPTUOUS, CONTEMPTIBLE

A *contemptuous* person is one who shows contempt for *others,* who is disdainful of them; a *contemptible* person or action is one deserving *our* contempt.

A cad would be even more *contemptible* if he were also *contemptuous.*

### CONTINUAL, CONTINUOUS

A *continuous* performance might be *continually* interrupted by a drunkard in the audience.

*Continuous*—without a break
*Continual*—recurring periodically

## CREDULOUS, CREDIBLE, CREDITABLE

A *credible* performance is a believable one, while a *creditable* performance does the actor credit and is therefore praiseworthy.

A *credulous* person is gullible, believing everything he hears. News can be *incredible* but a person is *incredulous.*

## DEDUCE, DEDUCT

You *deduce* something from the evidence given; you *deduct* contributions from your income tax.

*Deduce*—to infer, draw a conclusion
*Deduct*—to draw on your bank account

*Avoid:*

> From her foreign accent and her languid behavior, I was able to deduct that she was a spy. (Correct: *deduce*)

## DEFENDANT, PLAINTIFF

A *defendant* has to *defend* himself in court against charges brought by the *plaint*iff who makes the com*plaint.*

## DEFINITE, DEFINITIVE

A *definite* statement is specific and concrete; a *definitive* statement is final and conclusive, the last word on the subject. A *definitive* biography is so complete that no further biographies seem necessary.

## DEPRECATE, DEPRECIATE

To *deprecate* an action is to disapprove of it, generally because it is injurious to one's own cause. (Literally it means to pray down—Latin *precari,* to pray. The word *precarious,* for instance, describes a situation in which praying is of the essence.)

To *depreciate* (here the root *prec* comes from a Latin word meaning *price*) is to belittle, to lessen in value—opposed to *appreciate* which means to value properly or to increase in value.

Few writers pay any attention to this distinction, using *deprecate* and especially *deprecatory* instead of *depreciate* and *depreciatory.*

## DIALECT, DIALOGUE

A *dialect* is a local variation of a language. *Dialogue* is the technical script name for conversation, words exchanged between two or more people.

All plays are written in *dialogue;* some *dialogues* are written in *dialect.* The word *dialogue* has become a vogue word to mean something more formal than a conversation, less formal than a debate, and probably less boring than a conference. What's more, it guarantees an exchange of ideas which none of the other words do, and so it contributes a little something extra.

## DISINTERESTED, UNINTERESTED

To be *disinterested* is to be without self-interest, therefore, impartial; to be *uninterested* is to be bored or indifferent.

During a trial a good judge should be a *disinterested* but not an *uninterested* listener.

Despite the frequent use of *disinterested* for *uninterested* by many writers, 93 percent of the Usage Panel termed it "unacceptable."

## ENORMITY, ENORMOUSNESS

*Enormity* emphasizes the abnormality (the enormity of his crime); *enormousness* emphasizes the hugeness.

I never realized the enormity and rich variety of this land of almost 200 million people. (Preferred: *enormousness, immensity,* or *great size*)

## ENTOMOLOGY, ETYMOLOGY

*Entomology* is the study of insects; *etymology* is the study of words and their derivations.

## FACTIOUS, FACTITIOUS, FICTITIOUS

*Factious*—putting one's party first (*fact*ions)
*Factitious*—artificial (manu*fact*ured)
*Fictitious*—not true, made up (*fict*ion)

## FAMOUS, NOTORIOUS

Both mean well known, but *notorious* is used only in an unfavorable sense.

## FARTHER, FURTHER

For indicating distance, some people insist on *farther*, using *further* only when the meaning is *more*. Most of us use *further*, quite correctly, for all meanings.

> I can walk no *farther* or *further*. (either)
> I will discuss this no *further*. (only)
> Expect no further aid from me. (only)

## FLAUNT, FLOUT

To *flaunt* means to make a show or display of; to *flout* means to express contempt for, to defy. Webster III records *flaunt* as a synonym for *flout*. Such use of *flaunt* is rejected by 91 percent of the Usage Panel.

*Avoid:*

> In their new picture the Warners are flaunting tradition in a most entertaining way. (Correct: *flouting*)

### FORMALLY, FORMERLY

*Formally* refers to manner; *formerly*, to time.

### FORCEFUL, FORCIBLE

*Forceful* means vigorous, effective, dynamic.
*Forcible* means accomplished by the use of force.

### FORTUITOUS, FORTUNATE

Fortuitous means "accidental," "by chance."

Webster III gives "lucky" as one of the definitions of *fortuitous*. The Usage Panel by a vote of 85 percent finds this use of *fortuitous* to mean "lucky" or "fortunate" unacceptable.

### IMPLY, INFER

To *imply* is to suggest indirectly, hint at, even insinuate; to *infer* is to deduce, to draw a conclusion. In general the speaker *implies;* the listeners *infer*.

> Asked if he meant that Jordan would have to prevent the Palestinians from attacking Israel during the cease-fire period, Ambassador Rabin replied: "You can imply that."

Did the Ambassador really mean to say, "You can infer that"? Or was he the astute diplomat turning back a question with an equivocal, "You said it. I didn't."

Generally, the error made is to use *infer* where *imply* is correct.

> Do you mean to *infer* that I am telling a lie? (Correct: *imply*)

## LEAVE, LET

*To let* means to permit.

*To leave* means to allow to remain.

*Let me out* means *Permit me to go out* or, in other words, *I want to get out.*

*Leave me out* means *Allow me to remain out* or, in other words, *Don't include me.*

*Avoid:*

> *Leave* go of my arm. *Leave* George do it. He *left* me go. (Correct: *let*)

## LIE, LAY

Even writers confuse and misuse these two verbs more than any others in the English language.* A third verb, *to lie,* meaning to tell an untruth, merely adds to the confusion already existing between *to lie,* meaning to recline or to rest, and *to lay,* meaning to place or put down an object. The fact that other forms of these verbs overlap makes things worse. Watch carefully:

| | | | |
|---|---|---|---|
| PRESENT: | I lie (recline) | I lay (place) | I lie (untruth) |
| PAST: | I lay | I laid | I lied |
| PRESENT PERFECT: | I have lain | I have laid | I have lied |

* At a conference of teachers of English some years ago, a Southern novelist was invited to be the speaker. She opened her talk with, "I don't know why you asked me to address a group like this. Why I don't even know the difference between *lie* and *lay.* My characters always sit or stand. People in my stories just never get a rest."

*Correct:* I am lying in the sun.
*Correct:* Now I lay me down to sleep.
*Correct:* I laid my head on his shoulder.

Notice that while *lie* is never followed by an object, *lay,* meaning to place, always needs an object to complete it.

*Avoid:*

The hat was laying near the curb. (Correct: *lying*)
I laid on the beach all morning. (Correct: *lay*)

This little bit of advice may be of some help to you. Very often the verb *lie* can be replaced by a form of the verb *to be*. Here's the way it works.

The book l*ies* on the desk. (*is* on the desk)
The book l*ay* there yesterday. (w*as*)
The book has lai*n* there all week. (has bee*n*)

Before you attempt the exercise that follows, here's an example of a sentence that is correct, found in a note left for the milkman one morning: "Dear Mr. Milkman: Please lay a dozen eggs for me in the milk box."

### EXERCISE

(All the sentences that follow appeared in print or were spoken by someone on radio or television. And every time the wrong verb was used! You can do better.)

1. A battered marble head that had been (lying, laying) forgotten in the dust and gloom of the British Museum in London since 1859 has been identified as that of the Aphrodite of Cnidus, carved by Praxiteles in the fourth century B.C.

2. I was so overwhelmed when I saw the ball in the cup after a 260-yard wood shot from the fairway that I just (lay, laid) down on the green completely speechless.

3. Don't churn acid. Do you (lie, lay) awake when you want to sleep?

4. These new submarines can (lie, lay) on the bottom in 600 feet of water and stay there for weeks and weeks.

5. Two men who found $239,000 in cash (lying, laying, lieing) along a country road were rewarded today for their honesty with $2,700 from the grateful company.

6. Thus the Pathet Lao can be expected to (lie, lay) low when its troublemaking stirs the West to speak of diplomatic intervention or military aid to the beleaguered government.

7. Obviously satisfied, he (lay, laid) down his welding torch.

8. He told how the police (had laid, had lain) in ambush for him and two companions in their apartment in Bilbao.

9. One reason is to eliminate any deposit or sediment that might have collected in the bottle as it (lay, laid) on its side through the years.

10. I was amazed in round eight, when Ali (lay, laid) back against the ropes, making Frazier look like an amateur.

11. The general agreed that morale had been hurt because "so many wounded were (lying, laying, lieing) around waiting to be picked up."

### LIKE, AS

In 1957 Clifton Fadiman in an essay called "How to Speak Videomatic Televenglish" wrote:

> I am no Drew Pearson but I prophesy that within five years the man who boldly defends the heresy that *like* is not a conjunction will become the proper object of scrutiny by the Federal Bureau of Investigation.

Clifton Fadiman did not know then that a television commercial in the year 1970 was going to ask its listeners, "What do you want, good grammar or good taste?" This repeated question made many listeners, writers among them, so self-conscious that they looked with suspicion on any use of *like*.

Sentences like *The diamond was not really shaped* AS *a baseball diamond* appeared. The only word to use here is LIKE, which is both good grammar and good taste.

Grammatically, *as* is almost always a conjunction and normally introduces a clause *(Mr. Stevens visits cultural outposts as a general visits the front)* and *like* is a preposition normally followed by a noun or pronoun, not by a clause. *(There's no friend* LIKE *an old friend.)*

That's grammar, but usage is leaning toward *like* as a conjunction in certain constructions. On a TV talk show a U.S. senator said, "Nations behave very much like individuals do." Why not stop before *do* and get "Nations behave very much LIKE individuals"? He might also have said, "Nations behave very much AS individuals do." In other words, in the first example *like* is used as a preposition with *individuals* as the object, and in the second example *as* is used as a conjunction and introduces a clause.

But perhaps you have noticed that *like* is a stronger word than *as,* which by the way has several other meanings (see pp. 120–21). *Tell it like it is* has a mystique of its own. It is an accepted cliché. *Tell it as it is* is weak, ambiguous, not quite the same in meaning.

To be grammatically correct, you cannot always substitute *as* for *like.* Do you prefer *They dance* AS *other people breathe* to *They dance* LIKE *other people breathe?* If your answer is "I don't like either," you have a point. Obviously, the sentence is much improved by saying, "They dance AS EASILY AS other people breathe."

Therefore, it is not only a question of choosing AS instead of LIKE. Sometimes you need *as if* or *as though,* sometimes *the way,* sometimes additional qualifying words as in *as easily as.*

In the exercise that follows you will sometimes have to use such expressions.

## EXERCISE ON LIKE AND AS

(Try to improve these sentences, all taken from newspapers or television.)

1. Only Bill Hagler performed like a major college player should.

2. New York, as most major cities, has found that the general public is very apathetic in helping get rid of junk cars.

3. Each time when behind in its nine games, Oklahoma came back to victory and late in the game today it looked like the Sooners might do it again.

4. We'll show you Rome like nobody can.

5. She is a tall, handsome woman and, as Marian Morehouse, was famous in her own right.

6. They could have spent the rest of their lives alone and trapped on this war-torn island like they were the only two people on earth.

7. Nobody will miss her like I will.

8. Our Ambassador said today that Lincoln, as we, hated intolerance.

9. It looks like we're not going to have time for another question.

10. A twenty-eight-mile wind swept across Buckeye Stadium and the athletes played like they were wearing gloves.

11. Some children in the large-city schools do not have experiences as those who live in some other places.

12. Sutter Avenue, like most of Brownsville, looked like it had been visited by war or riot long before the incident.

MATERIAL, MATERIEL

*Material* (n)—commercial term for goods of any kind.

*MateriEL*—military term for equipment, supplies.

MITIGATE, MILITATE

Mitigate: to make milder; lessen severity of.

Militate: to work against, fight against. (Related in origin to the words *militant* and *military,* from the Latin *miles,* a soldier.)

Several times, in print, I have come across the incorrect *mitigate against. Against* always follows militate.

*To mitigate* a punishment is to make it less severe.

Things that *militate* against one's advancement are those that work against it.

OCULIST, OPTICIAN, OPTOMETRIST

An *oculist* is a doctor who specializes in diseases of the eye. If you want to amaze but not necessarily delight your friends you may also refer to him as an *ophthalmologist,* which is the word always used by doctors.

An *optometrist* is one who measures refractions and therefore can prescribe glasses, while an *optician* is merely one who sells them.

PERSECUTE, PROSECUTE

To *persecute* is to plague, to bring suffering to; *to prosecute* is to bring court action against.

POUR, SPILL

*To pour* means to direct the flow of a liquid, while *to spill* means to allow it to run out accidentally.

*Avoid:*

> Spill another cup of coffee for Mr. Westerly. (Correct: *pour*)

PRACTICABLE, PRACTICAL

Something is *practicable* that can be put into practice, something that is workable or feasible. Something is *practical* that is suited to actual conditions or that is not theoretical.

A man can be *practical* (not a dreamer) but his project may not be *practicable.*

A suggestion may be both *practical* and *practicable.*

PRINCIPAL, PRINCIPLE

If we quote the disgusted pupil who said, "It's not the school I don't like, it's just the (principal, principle) of the thing!" we may spell the word either way, depending on which meaning is intended.

*Principal* may be an adjective or a noun. In either case it means chief: the *principal* reason, the *principal* of a school.

*Principle* (often *principles*) means a rule or rules of conduct. We say: It is against his *principles;* he is a man of *principle.* It may help you to associate the word "princi*ples*" with ru*les* of conduct.

PROPONENT, PROTAGONIST

It's just nice to know that *proponent* (not *protagonist*) is the opposite of *opponent.* In a novel or a play the principal character is the *protagonist* (Greek *proto,* "first").

RAISE, RISE

You have to *raise* something; a cake or the sun *rises.*

RECOMMEND, REFER

Perhaps you, too, have heard the nurse in a doctor's office ask a new patient, "And who *recommended* you to Dr. Blank?" The word that should be used is, of course, *referred,* for it is Dr. Blank who was *recommended,* not the patient.

When using the word in this way, remember that it's the expert who is *recommended* and that the person who wishes to consult the expert is *referred.*

### RESPECTABLY, RESPECTFULLY, RESPECTIVELY

*Respectably* means in a manner worthy of respect.

*Respectfully* means with respect for someone else.

*Respectively* refers to a series of items taken in regular order.

*In a letter avoid*

Yours respectively. (Correct: *Yours respectfully*)

### RESTIVE, RESTLESS

People in dictatorships are likely to be *restive,* impatient, or rebellious under repressive control. A *restless* person is one who cannot rest, who must always have something to do. *Restive* has the idea of *resist* in it.

### SCHOLAR, PUPIL

"How many scholars have you in your class, Miss Finch?"

"None. But I have forty-nine pupils and only thirty-five seats."

A *scholar* most often means a learned person generally devoting himself to research or other erudite activities; a *pupil* is one who each morning hopes the school building will burn down and each afternoon doesn't mind that it hasn't.

SENSUAL, SENSUOUS

A *sensuous* person receives intellectual pleasure from the beauty that reaches him through the senses; a *sensual* person seeks physical pleasure from what reaches him through the senses.

SET, SIT

You *set* something down; you *sit* down.

SPECIE, SPECIES

Sidney Smith (1771–1845), Dean of St. Paul's and famed as a wit, in his sermons often said very proudly and patriotically that the English were universally known for their generosity and for the love of their species. On one such occasion, the collection was particularly disappointing. Dean Smith thereupon hastily added that he had apparently made a mistake, for he should have said they were distinguished for the love of their specie.

Both *specie* and *species* are singular. *Specie* refers to hard currency, not folding money. *Species* indicates a distinct class or category (a strange *species* of birds, not *specie*).

STALACTITE, STALAGMITE

In a natural cave a stala*c*tite *c*omes down from the *c*eiling; a stala*g*mite *g*rows up from the *g*round.

TRANSPIRE, HAPPEN, OCCUR

Though dictionaries list *transpire* as a synonym for *occur* and *happen,* discriminating writers still use *transpire* in its original meaning of *becoming known gradually.*

It is still a pleasant shock to come across a sentence

like: *The hunters, it transpired, had found and marked some thirty hollow trees in different parts of the forest.* (Gerald Durrell)

### TURBID, TURGID

*Turbid* means muddy, roiled, clouded; *turgid* means swollen, inflated, pompous.

An author's writing may be either muddied (a *turbid* script) or pompous (a *turgid* style) or both. When water is muddy it is *turbid.*

### TYPEWRITER, TYPIST

The machine is a *typewriter;* the operator of the machine is a *typist.*

### VENAL, VENIAL

A *venal* act is a corrupt one, influenced by money. A *venial* sin is like a white lie—excusable or forgivable. Associating *venial* with *trivial* may help you to distinguish between the two.

## EXERCISE IN WORDS SOMETIMES CONFUSED

1. The Prime Minister indicated that Egyptians would neither expect nor *(except, accept)* Soviet military involvement in combat.

2. He *(borrowed, lent, loaned)* one hundred dollars from his brother-in-law.

3. There was disagreement *(among, between)* theater owners, restaurateurs, actors, and producers on how the new time (7:30 curtain instead of 8:30) will *(affect, effect)* business.

4. The wife of Eugene O'Neill—and this is hard to understand—was largely *(disinterested, uninterested)* in the theater.

5. Every wild life *(specie, species)* has its own characteristics.

6. If such a replacement should be *(affected, effected)* minorities would be seriously *(affected, effected).*

7. The Russians, apparently unwilling to show their hand at this time, are *(laying, lying)* low.

8. Please *(bring, take)* this book to the library for me.

9. The Center's choice of a fourth production was somewhat less *(fortuitous, fortunate)* than its predecessors.

10. The discovery of the laser beam may well be the *(climatic, climactic)* achievement of modern science.

11. In the main he regards the press and television as primarily *(complimentary, complementary)* rather than competitive.

12. *(Beside, Besides)* the three police officers whom he accused of negligence, the Commissioner *(implied, inferred)* that there were others equally culpable.

13. For comfort you put a wad of this specially prepared cotton between *(each toe, the toes).*

14. Mr. Anderson described the forthcoming trial as the *(climactic, climatic)* point of all dissent in America.

15. Some animals are able to *(adapt, adopt)* themselves very quickly to new surroundings.

16. There can be nothing but ultimate confusion and chaos if court decrees are *(flaunted, flouted)* whatever the pretext.

17. In so doing, these candidates *(imply, infer)* that their opponents have really no solution.

18. I say *(leave, let)* the world rock along yet awhile; there is yet much to marvel at, much to unravel.

19. The handicap of geography alone has *(militated, mitigated)* against adequate solutions for the problems of poverty, ignorance, and disease.

20. Earlier he was held in contempt for *(implying, inferring)* that the court was aiding and abetting the state.

21. The United States Ambassador's only advice to the tourist groups was not to *(flaunt, flout)* their wealth.

22. The existence of such a deposit of dense material has been revealed by its *(affect, effect)* on orbiting vehicles as they pass overhead.

23. The *(forceful, forcible)* shearing of forty long-haired men at a police station in a working-class suburb of Athens has resulted in a small political crisis.

24. In planning production of the Bible, Nelson fully realized the *(enormity, enormousness)* of the task.

25. He is a big-boned, heavyset man who wears a small beard and modest moustache, laughs easily, and is given to mild *(self-deprecation, self-depreciation)*.

26. "I hope that no parents, by their example, will teach their children to *(flaunt, flout)* the law," the school superintendent said.

27. The Secretary of Defense showed the newspapermen a rusty piece of oil pipe expecting them to *(imply, infer)* that it had been captured during the Laos offensive.

28. At best, pushing the pollution further offshore can only buy temporary relief for the Jersey coast. It will do nothing to *(militate, mitigate)* the progressive pollution of all the world's seas, a menace to the well-being of every coastal state and nation.

29. In the original script the hero was portrayed as a foolish *(venal, venial)* fellow interested only in looting and black-marketing.

30. From the evidence produced, no Sherlock Holmes was needed to *(deduce, deduct)* that he was a man of *(principal, principle).*

## HIS VERSUS THEIR

*His* is singular; it refers to one person.

*Their* is plural; it refers to more than one.

But words like *everyone, everybody, anyone, anybody* confuse the issue.

In a sentence like "Everyone in the room jumped to *(his, their)* feet," we face a problem. Some will argue that since there are many people in the room, the word used should be *their.* But strict grammarians shake their heads. "No," they say. "You don't say, 'Everyone *are* in the room'; you say, 'everyone *is* in the room.' Therefore, the word to be used is the singular, *his,* and so 'Everyone jumped to *his* feet' is right."

The Women's Liberation Movement has its own ideas on the subject. In a debate with William F. Buckley, Jr., held at Cambridge University in February 1973, Germaine Greer at one point in her presentation said: "I would have thought that everyone here regardless of their sex, his sex —I beg your pardon. . . ." Her apologetic switch to strict grammatical rules was pointedly sarcastic. *His* indeed!

So if you want to be strictly grammatical use *his* when the word *his* looks back to *everybody, everyone,* etc. If you want to avoid the problem altogether, use *all those in the room.* That's always plural: *All those in the room jumped to* their *feet.*

Chapter 9

# Words: Fragile! Handle with Care!

### THEY JUST DON'T SPEAK ENGLISH HERE

Richmond, Va., May 19—Karl Archibald, a Londoner, was telling friends his confusion at American word usage. He dwelt on the word "fix":

"I am invited to dinner and my host asks how I would like a drink fixed. He means mixed. My hostess calls us to hurry because dinner is all fixed —and she means prepared. My host says he must get a flat tire fixed—and he means repaired.

"You say you are on a fixed income. You mean steady and unchanged. You say you will fix something to the wall—you mean attach. And you say you'll 'fix him'—and you mean get revenge.

"Finally you remark that you are in 'a hell of a fix,' and I see that you may have some comprehension of my predicament in trying to follow your simplification."

—*New York Post*

Years ago when travel to Europe was by steamship only, those on board used to be regaled each day with a copy of the ship's paper. The most interesting reading was not so much the news but the advertisements of European health resorts. One such advertisement fascinated me then. The years have not robbed it of its charm.

### SANATORY OBERWALD NEAR ST. GALL

Always open and visited for winter and spring cures very liked. Two approved physicians and one female

> physician. Also for reconvalescents and adopted especially for finishing cure. In autumn fruit and grapes cure. In winter inure and winter-sport cures.
>
> Best success of cure at even all diseases. (Non accepted are Tuberculosis and mad injured.) Special part for femal diseases.
>
> Even one doesn't know if there is to be preferred picturesque lakescape or the grandiose high-mountains and then it is again the changing richly formed foreground which makes the whole to a unique, the senses so refreshing landscape.
>
> Marks 10–18 already on staying of 3 days.

What's wrong with it? It contains English words and there aren't any errors in grammar that you can point your finger at. Yet it isn't English as we know it. Its peculiarities are not the peculiarities of English but of some other language. That's what's wrong with it.

For each language has its own peculiar way of saying things. You can't just carry words over bodily from one language to another. You can't translate words; you have to translate meaning. An American correspondent in Moscow found that out when he tried to send his report to his newspaper. In his story, he wrote that the American Ambassador "stood within a stone's throw of Stalin." The Moscow censor raged at him for his colossal rudeness. Finally, when the reporter was permitted to explain what the American expression really meant, the censor said, "Oh, in that case we change it. We change it to read like this: 'The American Ambassador stood near Stalin. He threw *no* stones!' "

When we respect the peculiarities of a language, when we remain faithful to its word order, we are speaking it *idiomatically*.

This chapter will deal with some of the characteristics of *idiomatic* English, pointing out pitfalls in our path.

None of us would say "best success of cure at even all diseases," but there are less obvious traps, set by prepositions, that we sometimes walk into. Because prepositions are especially treacherous we start with them.

## PREPOSITIONS

However, there's one thing you don't have to worry about. One of the popular misconceptions about prepositions is that you should not end a sentence with a preposition. Ridiculous! Here's one with five:

> Little Johnny complained to his mother as she sat down to read to him: "What did you bring that book I didn't want to be read to out of up for?"

In a very successful comedy—*Forget-Me-Not Lane*—the father, a comic, straitlaced character, solemnly, like Polonius, gives his son this advice: "Never tell a lie. Never be unfaithful to your family and to your friends. And never end a sentence with a preposition."

Later on in an angry exchange with his father, the son asks, "What are your sleeves rolled up for?" A stern look appears on Dad's face. His son promptly rephrases his sentence to: "Up for what are your sleeves rolled?" His father is all smiles.

Well, you can be all smiles too. Don't worry about ending a sentence with a preposition. Sometimes it is the better way; sometimes it's the only way:

*It's a good rule to go by* is certainly better than *It's a good rule by which to go.*

*What it's all about.* Try to say this by tucking in the preposition somewhere *within* the sentence. Almost impossible!

Winston Churchill nailed this nonsense down when he

once retorted with, "That is something up with which I shall not put."

## IDIOMATIC PHRASES

Occasionally these pesky little prepositions cling like barnacles to certain verbs, adjectives, or nouns. These clinging prepositions sometimes have become fused with these words into an indestructible idiom. Often there is no rhyme or reason for urging the use of one preposition rather than another Some of the most frequent idiomatic uses are given here along with misuses sometimes heard:

accepted *at* or *by* (not *to* a college)
accompanied *by* (preferred to *with*, when speaking of persons)
adapted *for* (meaning *suited to*)
adapted *from* (meaning *changed from*)
adapted *to* (meaning *adjusted to*)
arrive *at* or *in* (not *to*)
*at* someone's home (rather than *over, up, by*)
coincide *with* (not *on*)
deals *with* (rather than *about*)
deprived *of* (not *from*)
destructive *of* (rather than *to*)
different *from* (although *than* is coming up strong; see page 116)
discourage them *from attacking* (not *to make an attack*)
forbid you *to do this* (not *from doing this*)
*meanwhile* or *in the meantime* (not *in the meanwhile*)
identical *with* (rather than *to*)
in accordance *with* (not *to*)
inferior *to* (not *than*)
*in* my opinion (not *to*)
in relation *to* (not *with*)
in respect *to* (rather than *of*)

in search *of* (rather than *for*)
*off* (not *off of*)
preferable *to* (not *than*)
related *to* (not *with*)
similar *to* (not *with*)

## VERBS WITH PREPOSITIONS

There are many verbs which require a preposition to complete their meanings. Sometimes we incorrectly omit it. Here are some glaring examples.

### GRADUATE (FROM)

*Avoid:*

I graduated Abraham Lincoln High School. (Correct: *I graduated from*)

### OPERATE

This verb should be followed by *on* or *upon. To operate* alone means merely to work something. The word *surgery* is replacing *operation.*

*Avoid:*

My father is going to be operated this afternoon. (Correct: *operated on*)

### TEACHES

When the institution is mentioned, *at* or *in* should be used.

*Avoid:*

My brother-in-law teaches college, but my sister teaches high school. (Correct: *at college, in high school*)

## VERBS WITHOUT PREPOSITIONS

If there are some of us who omit a preposition where it is needed, there are others—probably the same ones—who put one in where it is wrong to do so. Again some glaring examples:

### ANNOUNCED

Takes a direct object without benefit of prepositions.

*Avoid:*

He announced about the important meeting to be held on Monday.

### DISCUSSED

Always needs a direct object.

*Avoid:*

We discussed about world affairs for hours.

It is always better to follow this verb with some direct object. It sounds a bit awkward to say: "We sat up all night and discussed."

### JOIN or MEET

These words are better off without prepositions.

The Cambodian army's objective was to join up with the forces of South Vietnam. (Why not just *join?*)

*Avoid:*

We met up with some delightful people at that party.

### MENTION

Is always followed by a direct object.

*Avoid:*

Don't mention about what I told you.

### COMPARE TO or WITH

When the comparison is an actual one (between things in the same category) *with* is a slight preference.

In the sentence *The Senator compared our missile capability with Russia's* the word *with* is preferred, although *to* is widely used.

However, when the comparison is a poetic one—a simile—only *to* should be used. Shakespeare begins one of his sonnets with: "Shall I compare thee *to* a summer's day?"

### DIFFERENT FROM, DIFFERENT THAN

*Different than* is now found so frequently in print that concessions must be made to its use, especially where *than* saves words or avoids an awkward construction.

> The enforcement of the First Amendment has a different meaning today *than* at the end of the eighteenth century.

(If *from* were used, you would have to write *from the one it had.*)

> Statistics indicate that the propaganda scales are weighted these days somewhat differently *than* popularly imagined.

(There's really no smooth way of writing this sentence with *from* unless you prefer the awkward *from what is popularly imagined.*)

However, when a prepositional phrase (preposition and object) follows immediately after different, *from* is to be preferred to *than*. Here are some examples:

> Give complete address if different *from* the above.
> He is different *from* me in every way.
> The TV version is using a cast different *from* the off-Broadway version.

## REPEATING THE PREPOSITION FOR CLARITY

Often in order to make a sentence absolutely clear it is wise to repeat the preposition when there are several parallel phrases connected by *than* or *as well as*.

1. Craig's wife thought more of her home than her husband.
2. Craig's wife thought more of her home than of her husband.

Both statements happen to be true, but the first means that Mr. Craig thought less of his home than his wife did, whereas the second sentence means that her home meant more to Mrs. Craig than her husband did. Repeating a preposition will often avoid ambiguity.

> He looks better in a bathing suit than a tuxedo. (Clearer: *than in a tuxedo*)

When phrases in series are suspended, no prepositions should be dropped.

> I am in favor (of), not opposed to, the bill.
> The article gives stimulation (to) and actual practice in . . .

## OVERUSED COMPOUND PREPOSITIONS

### AS TO

There is a tendency to make this an all-service preposition. Often a more appropriate preposition may be used or *as to* may be left out altogether.

> He had peculiar notions *as to* one's rights in a democracy. (Preferred: *about one's rights*)

*Apropos of* is also an abused expression. It is often a pompous way of saying *about.*

*Avoid:*

> He was sarcastic *apropos* my tennis playing. (This is a double fault, for the expression is *apropos of* and even then it is a pompous substitute for the more accurate preposition, *about.*)

### IN CONNECTION WITH

Generally the simple preposition *on* or *about* is more effective and less affected.

> He wanted to have a long talk with me *in connection with* my future. (Preferred: *about*)
> The legislature ought to do something *in connection with* eliminating pollution. (Preferred: *about eliminating*)

### (OF) THE FACT THAT

Except when it comes at the beginning of a sentence, this phrase can usually be cut down to *that.*

> We were not certain *of the fact that* he was coming. (Preferred: *that he was coming*)
> He should have been told *of the fact that* deductions can be made for medical expenses. (Preferred: *that deductions,* etc.)

## SUPERFLUOUS WORDS

Have you friends who are doctors or dentists who begin a story with, "I have a patient of mine"? Do you point out to them that they are repeating an idea, that when they say *I have a patient* they don't need to add *of mine,* or that they can simply say "a patient of mine"?

In each of the following sentences one or more words can be omitted because they are unnecessary or repeat an idea already there.

*Example:* This here book (Omit *here*)

1. If all of us cooperate together, we'll get somewhere.

2. He sold ties, socks, shirts, and etc.

3. The purpose of this resolution is to get people off of the welfare rolls and back into productive activities.

4. He was guilty of a false misstatement.

5. It was the general consensus of opinion that war was inevitable.

6. They had nothing in common with each other.

7. A seat off the aisle would be more preferable.

8. Asked as to what effect this would have on inflation, he replied very briefly.

9. He shook his fist as he rose up to speak.

10. I am enclosing herewith a check for fifty dollars.

11. After the catch Harrelson returned back to first base.

12. He must now realize the fact that we are no longer able to help him.

13. I typed up three copies of the contract in about five minutes.

14. I must first do this before I go.

15. It all happened at 4:30 P.M. in the afternoon.

16. He carefully examined each and every entry.

17. He immediately placed the business on a more sounder basis.

18. In my opinion, I think the situation has grown worse.

19. In spite of tremendous losses the offensive continued on with unabated fury.

20. The smoking of a Harvester cigar is a pleasure reserved exclusively for men only.

21. I have a friend of mine who always goes there.

22. His score for eighteen holes never exceeded more than 75.

23. He should have been told of the fact that deductions are made for lateness as well as for absence.

24. In the meanwhile, the operator cut us off.

25. It made people wonder as to what he was going to do next.

26. He was miraculously restored back to health.

27. I will let you know later whether or not I can attend the dinner.

28. He was elected unanimously by all the members.

29. I am not sure as to whom I shall vote for.

30. He is now at work on a biography of Florence Nightingale's life.

## TROUBLESOME WORDS

### AS

*As* is best used in comparisons or in the sense of *at the same time*. Any other use must be viewed with suspicion.

It should not be used instead of *that.*

*Avoid:*

> I don't know *as* he wants to. (Correct: *that* or *whether*)
> I'm not sure as *how* he can do better. (Correct: *that* or *whether)*

*As* is a weak substitute for *because* or *since.*

> My father, a student at the University, did not complete his studies *as* he enlisted in the 1914 war.

How much more precise *because* would be!

> I left the party early, *as* I was not having a good time. (Preferred: *because* or *since*)

Don't use *as* alone to introduce an enumeration. Don't be afraid to use *like.*

> I prefer stories *as* "The Tell-Tale Heart" and "The Black Cat." (Preferred: *stories such as, such stories as,* or *like*)

TYPE

Don't omit the *of* after type.

*Avoid:*

> Our soap is especially designed for that type beauty. (Preferred: that *type of beauty*)
> There is opportunity in the defense industries for that type man. (Preferred: that *type of man*)

(Ninety-four percent of the Usage Panel found this use of *type* without *of* unacceptable!)

## FOR THE WASTEBASKET

The following words are strictly for the wastebasket or whatever is handy! They have no reason for being.

### ANYWAYS, ANYWHERES, SOMEWHERES, EVERYWHERES

There should be no S at the end of any of these words.

*Avoid:*

> It's a long *ways* from here. (Correct: *way*)

### BEING THAT

Don't use *being that* or *being as how* to express a causal idea. *Since* will express the idea adequately.

*Avoid:*

> *Being that* he was in the city, we decided to meet him there. (Correct: *Since* he was in the city, etc.)

### COULD OF, WOULD OF

In speaking, this error is not noticeable; in writing, it is a sign of illiteracy. If you want to indicate that someone is using the contracted form, write *could've, would've,* etc.

### EXSETERA (and so forth)

The word is *et cetera* (Latin for *and other things*).

### ENLARGEN

No such word. Use *enlarge.*

### ENTHUSED

Not really a wastebasket word—just a pet prejudice. (Seventy-two percent of the Usage Panel found it unacceptable.) Say: He was enthusiastic about.

HAD OUGHT, HADN'T OUGHT

> *Correct:* He ought to have done it.
> *Correct:* He ought not to have done it.
> "He *hadn't ought to* lead this country down the road to war." (Correct: He *ought not to have* led, etc.)

IN or WITH REGARDS TO

If you wish, you can close a letter with "With regards to Aunt Minnie," but for the phrase meaning *in reference to* you must use *in regard to* or *with regard to.*

> In regards to the matter you talked about last night, I wish, etc. (Correct: *in regard to, with regard to,* or *as regards,* omitting *to*)

IRREGARDLESS

No such word. The objection to *irregardless* is seen more clearly in the word *unmerciless.* The prefix *un* means *not* and the suffix *less* means *without,* so that the word—if it existed, which it does not—would mean not without mercy. *Merciless* is correct. So is *regardless.*

MOMENTO

Please! The word is *memento,* something to remember a person or occasion by—even though Webster III lists *momento* as a variant.

PORTENTIOUS

No such word! The word is *portentous.*

PRESUMPTIOUS

No such word. Throw it away and use *presumptuous.*

### PROPHESIZE

No such word! The verb is *prophesy* (sigh); the noun is *prophecy* (see).

### SECONDHANDED

No such word. Use *secondhand.*

### UNDOUBTABLY

*Undoubtedly* wrong.

### UNEQUIVOCABLY

*Unequivocally* wrong!

## EXERCISE ON IDIOMS

Improve the following sentences:

1. In our English class we discussed about world affairs.

2. Being that it was raining we stood home.

3. Yes, he did mention about the trip you are going to take.

4. The official spokesman compared the enemy airplanes with a swarm of locusts.

5. Recently she was accepted to the University of Wisconsin.

6. In Alabama Blacks have repeatedly accused the registration board of Montgomery County with discrimination.

7. An average smoker can expect to lose five and one-half years of his life as compared to a nonsmoker.

8. No all-star game has produced so many hitters who have fashioned as many home runs by midseason than this one.

9. I'm glad I got that off of my mind.

10. She is the only girl in the large cast who looks old enough to have graduated high school.

11. The avowed purpose of this bill is to take people off of welfare and put them in productive activities.

12. The new site is within five miles from the old one.

13. He entered the army on November 1970.

14. There's very little more to say in regards to that matter.

15. My cousin is going to the hospital to be operated tomorrow.

## SOME TROUBLESOME CONCEPTS

In order to speak English idiomatically we have to respect not only the grammatical rules of the language but the habits that have been formed through many years of use. Some of the problems in which language habits—not grammar—must be our guides are taken up here.

Although two negatives do not ordinarily make an affirmative,* they do make an embarrassing situation for anyone who wants to write or speak English correctly. The following headline from *The New York Times* of November 19, 1965,

> DOUBLE NEGATIVE TRAPS THIEF
> WHO SOUGHT ALMS IN A NOTE

shows other trouble one can get into! Most of us instinctively shy away from sentences like:

> He ain't no piccolo player. (Correct: *is no* or *isn't a*)

* One of the exceptions is the singing commercial: "Everybody doesn't like something, / But nobody doesn't like Sara Lee."

That don't make no difference. (Correct: *doesn't make any*)

He isn't never coming here no more. (Correct: *ever . . . any more*)

There are, however, other double negatives not so obvious as these, which should nevertheless be avoided. Don't use a negative verb with *hardly, scarcely, neither, only,* or *but* (meaning *only*).

*Avoid:*

1. They don't hardly do any work. (Correct: *do hardly any*)
2. I won't scarcely have time. (Correct: *I'll scarcely*)
3. Hardly no people play here mornings. (Correct: *hardly any*)
4. I don't believe in it neither. (Correct: *either*)

## EXERCISE IN CORRECTION OF DOUBLE NEGATIVES

In correcting the following sentences don't do what one bright boy did when asked to correct *She didn't know nothing about nothing.* He rewrote the sentence and came up with: *She was completely ignorant.*

All you need to do is to get rid of the word or words that double the negative idea.

1. He hasn't hardly a friend left.

2. The rest are left to wander in the lowlands of West Bengal without hardly a trace of food or shelter.

3. He wasn't scarcely three years old when his parents decided his future for him.

4. I haven't seen neither his brother nor him.

5. Because of the snow I haven't been out of the house only once since Christmas.

6. No state nowhere would allow such a situation to exist.

7. From a booklet given to American forces in North Africa: "You must not talk to Moslem women. Under no circumstances."

8. The Italian government warned tonight that, unless adequate aid were not tendered at once to that country, a real crisis might result.

9. The government's reluctance is based on doubts that the former Vietcong would not be trustworthy.

10. At this time I would not like to see Congress limit the restrictions on bombing Cambodia.

Numbers 8, 9, and 10 take a little time to figure out. They are "double takes" like what the owner of a summer adult camp said when a performance scheduled for 8:30 had not yet begun at 9:00. He was heard to ask in an angry stage whisper, "What's holding up the delay?"

## PARALLEL STRUCTURE

It is not too much to expect stylistically that when several items are connected by the coordinating conjunctions *and, or, but, nor* the same constructions be used for all the items.

For example, the sentence *She was required to take dictation, to type letters, and filing all correspondence* is a little jarring on the ears because *and filing all correspondence* breaks the structural sequence. It would be better to keep all of the items parallel and end the sentence with *and to file all correspondence.*

Improve the sentences in the following exercise.

## EXERCISE IN PARALLEL STRUCTURE

1. Dr. Stockmann had the choice of giving up his ideals and principles or to remain faithful to them.

2. His style is clear, sparkling, and a delight to read.

3. On his European trip, the President motored through downtown Madrid, and rural Irish towns, consulted with American diplomats, visited the graves of ancestors, and placing a wreath at a monument to the Yugoslav Unknown Soldier.

4. Modern novelists have two common weaknesses: first, a lack of philosophy; and second, they are obsessed by a need to reproduce contemporary life with almost photographic accuracy.

5. Contestants were also required to dance to both rock and waltz rhythms and explaining why they liked their jobs.

6. Please explain why you left your former college, why you wish to attend this one, and your academic and professional goals.

7. The foundations give large grants to aid institutions of learning, to promote research, and for various human needs.

8. There comes a time in every nation's history when that nation must begin to question why it exists, for whom it exists, and changes necessary in order to insure its future existence.

## FIRST AID!

> The word Jack Benny uses most is *marvelous.* Everything he likes and describes is *marvelous.* When he was in vaudeville he used this adjective to describe almost every act. A letter he received from a fan caused him to be careful how he used the word. The letter read: "Enjoyed your performance very much. Like everything about you but the word

> *marvelous*. Am sending you a list of words you can use in the place of *marvelous*. Except for that, Mr. Benny, you are *marvelous*."*

The word *marvelous* is not like the words we've just talked about, which fill meaningless gaps, because you need it or some other descriptive word. It's just overworked and exhausted, and what we need for it and other catchall words is a first-aid kit of fresher, more exact words that can take its place.

### First-Aid Kit for Overworked Words

For a change try these:

marvelous—pleasant, beautiful, superb, excellent, magnificent, amazing, thrilling, fine, agreeable, skillful (depending on the shade of meaning you want)

groovy—delightful, entertaining, amusing, charming, excellent, magnificent

nice—beautiful, fine, pleasant, agreeable, charming

awfully—very, remarkably, unusually, unbelievably, exceedingly

OK—all right, certainly, very well, surely, fine, yes, of course

lousy—Some years ago, a Brooklyn man wrote to the editor of one of the tabloids: "Your editorials are masterpieces of insipid, stupid, inane, corrupt, demagogic, bigoted, dishonest, putrid, rotten, despicable, poverty-stricken, low-down, unmitigated, pestiferous, peerless and matchless yellow journalism, charlatanry, bamboozling, and flimflam."

On the subject of overused words, *U.S. News & World Report* of August 9, 1971, has an article containing this interesting statement:

* Sidney Skolsky in the *New York Post*.

The Nixon speech writers have been told to avoid such words as "viable," "meaningful," and "relevant." Explanation from a White House source: "These are among the vogue words of the so-called intellectual set and they have taken on trite and pretentious stature."

## TRITE EXPRESSIONS—CLICHÉS

There are other expressions which were once colorful and fresh but which constant use has robbed of some of their luster and made stale. We call such expressions trite or hackneyed. *Trite* literally means rubbed; that is, rubbed threadbare or having the shine rubbed off. A hackney is a hired horse, and a hackneyed expression is one that is as overworked as such a horse usually is.

This doesn't mean that such expressions are never to be used. Often, clichés are a shortcut to communication and though a bit tarnished are nevertheless useful. You just don't want to use them too often.

If you overburden your conversation or correspondence with such expressions as those listed here, your writing will lack freshness, individuality, sincerity—and suspense.

### A Partial List of Trite Expressions

*a battle royal
a good time was had by all
all sorts and conditions
as luck would have it
*beggars description
better late than never
bolt from the blue
breathed a sigh of relief
busy as a bee
by hook or by crook
by leaps and bounds
checkered career
conspicuous by his absence
cut to the quick

*dance attendance on
*do justice to the meal
*doomed to disappointment
*favor us with a song
few and far between
*fill a long-felt want
from the ridiculous to the sublime
galore—flowers galore, fellows galore, etc.
in the last analysis
in this day and age
irony of fate
it goes without saying
it's a small world after all
last but not least
life and limb
my better half
nipped in the bud
none the worse for wear
no sooner said than done
no time like the present
*point with pride
*poor but honest
*proud possessor
*reigns supreme
senses reeled
snare and a delusion
sticks out like a sore thumb
take a dim view of
to all intents and purposes
too numerous to mention
trials and tribulations
view with alarm
*wended our way home
Words fail me

Nevertheless, you can see that many of the expressions given here are at times clearly unavoidable.* But those

* Trying to avoid "like a bolt from the blue," a journalist describing a situation that suddenly became a near riot has just come up with: "like a bolt of lightning from a clear sky." Maybe it's better to go along with rather than around clichés.

starred, which are either pompous, stilted, bookish, or outdated, should be avoided *like the plague* (another useful cliché).

And if you do use a cliché, at least get it right. Here are a number I have collected over the years. Rewrite them correctly.

### Malclichés
### Overheard Over the Years

1. I slept like a lark.
2. He has it down to a pat.
3. The burglar struck her and she fell down with a thug.
4. They're as alike as three peas in a porridge.
5. He's rotten to the cork.
6. He and my husband were childish friends.
7. This biography is interesting, not cut and dry like some others I've read.
8. He behaved like a bull in a china closet.
9. It's an error to be human.
10. The fog was so thick it was like a knife.
11. My husband's so busy. He's working like a Trojan horse.
12. I never take airplanes. I like to be on terra cotta.
13. She sticks to him like a leash.
14. She burnt the candle with both hands.
15. That's the whole thing in a bombshell.

## CHOICE OF WORDS

At this point you may well feel like asking, "Look. If we're going to avoid all the words and expressions listed in this chapter, what's left?" Roughly about half a million words. From among them you can choose those words that will express your thoughts best. And choosing the right word is a real achievement. The long-suffering customer who answered the headwaiter's question, "Have you given your order?" with, "Yes, but please make it an entreaty," spoke with a feeling for words made keener by hunger.

Many of us, instead of learning how to use the simple, familiar words effectively, go off in search of long words or strange words, thinking to improve our speech and writing in that way.

Do you remember Wilkins Micawber? The first words Mr. Micawber ever spoke to David Copperfield—David was only nine then—were: "Under the impression that your travels in these parts of the metropolis have not yet been extensive, I shall be happy to call this evening and install you in the knowledge of the nearest way." What he meant was: "Since you don't know much about the city, I'll be glad to show you about this evening."

Writing in 1876, William Matthews, professor of English literature at the University of Chicago, deplored the use of pretentious "swelling words and phrases" and told this anecdote:

> "Never, perhaps, did a college professor give a better lesson in rhetoric than was given by a plain farmer in Kennebec County, Maine, to a schoolmaster. 'You are excavating a subterranean channel, it seems,' said the pedagogue, as he saw the farmer at work near his house. 'No, sir,' was the reply, 'I am only digging a ditch.' "*

* From *Words, Their Use and Abuse* by William Matthews.

Long words merely make our speech pompous, flabby, or inaccurate. What then?

If you want to get rid of conversational B.O. (Boring Others) here are a few simple suggestions:

1. BE BRIEF. If you can say something effectively in ten words, don't use twenty-five or a hundred. One of the most desirable of all economies is the economy of words. Think of the music critic who wrote, "An amateur string quartet played Brahms here last evening. Brahms lost." Don't clutter up what you say with useless words. If you have a choice between a short word and a long one, choose the short one. It will usually convey your meaning more clearly and more vigorously.

2. BE SPECIFIC. A concrete word is always better than an abstract word. A specific detail is always better than a vague generality. A *yacht* or *tugboat* is better than a *ship* and "a dirty British coaster with a salt-caked smoke-stack" is best of all. It's John Masefield and it's concrete, specific, and vivid. Occasionally try to find words that make your listener see as well as hear what you are saying. And occasionally try to listen. It often shows a fine command of language to say nothing.

3. BE YOURSELF. Don't be afraid to be yourself. Don't be afraid to be natural. The most attractive thing to be is YOU.

## A FINAL WORD

If you want to write well, respect all the *don'ts* in this chapter and observe all the *do's*. Then add this bit of general advice: *Write the way you speak*—naturally and without affectation—with this important difference, that in writing you have time to think *before* you write and an opportunity to revise *after* you have written. If you do this, the result will be *you,* and that's worth all the long words in an unabridged dictionary and all the flowery words in a thesaurus.

When your conversation reaches new levels of vocabulary and gains greater flexibility, your writing will, too. And what's more important it will still be *genuinely* you, not an imitation.

Chapter 10

# Stop, Look, and Listen: Spelling

FOOTBALL PLAYER POOR IN SPELLING

Phoenix, Ariz. (AP)—Shanty Hogan, football coach at Phoenix Junior College, claims this is a true story.

He asked all of his freshman players to fill out a card in case of a serious injury. The card lists whom to notify and such information. One blank is for religion. One player wrote, "Bhaptizz."

Hogan chuckled and then asked the lad, "Now son, what religion are you?"

The boy answered, "Presbyterian."

"But you wrote Baptist," the coach said.

"I know," the player said, "but I can't spell Presbyterian."

—From AP dispatch

Unfortunately, our football candidate was born some three centuries too late, for strangely enough at one time spelling did depend on the whim and fancy of the speller. One authority tells us that Shakespeare spelled his name in some thirty different ways (Shakspere, Shakespeare, Shaxpere, Schackspere, Shaxpur being some of the more frequent variations). The grandson of James II, writing about his father, refers to him sometimes as Jems and at other times as Gems! Spelling was a grand and glorious free-for-all. You spelled the way words sounded to you, and it was almost a game to see in how many different ways you could achieve a recognizable word.

Even as late as 1764, James Boswell, famous biographer of Samuel Johnson, in a letter written to his friend William Temple, misspelled, according to our standards, the words *agreable, allready, stile* (style), *beleive, it's* (for its), *compleat, freind, immediatly, satisfy'd, english, nonsence, realy, smoak, yeild, corespond, chuse* (choose), *chearfull, allmost, releiving, sollicited, abhorr,* and *awefull.* If Boswell had consulted his friend's celebrated dictionary, published nine years earlier, he would have spelled all but two (*compleat* and *chuse* are given as variant spellings) as we spell them today. Twenty-one spelling mistakes in one letter! Poor Boswell! Miss Finch would never have let him pass in English 1.

Many attempts to reform English spelling have been made in the last one hundred years. M. T. Shields in a recent letter to *The Economist* reminds us that G. B. Shaw, among others, was one of the champions of spelling reform. Shaw suggested that one letter be changed or eliminated each year in order to give people time to adjust to the change. Shields' scenario is simplicity itself!

> For example, in Year 1 that useless letter "c" would be dropped to be replased by either "k" or "s," and likewise "x" would no longer be part of the alphabet. The only kase in which "c" would be retained would be the "ch" formation, which will be dealt with later. Year 2 might well reform "w" spelling, so that "which" and "one" would take the same konsonant, wile Year 3 might well abolish "y" replasing it with "i," and Iear 4 might fiks the "g-j" anomali wonse and for all.
>
> Jenerally, then, the improvement would kontinue iear bai iear, with Iear 5 doing awai with useless double konsonants, and Iears 6-12 or so modifaiing vowlz and the rimeining voist and unvoist konso-

nants. Bai Ier 15 or sou, it wud fainali bi posibl tu meik ius ov thi ridandant letez "c," "y" and "x"—bai now jast a memori in the maindz ov ould doderez—tu riplais "ch," "sh" and "th" rispektivli.

Fainali, xen, aafte sam 20 iers ov orxogrefkl riform, wi wud hev a lojikl, kohirnt speling in ius xrewawt xe Ingliy-spiking werld.

You can see how absurd this kind of spelling "improvement" can be. So there's no sense in sitting around on our inertia waiting for reforms. Let's roll up our sleeves and get to work.

## POWER OF OBSERVATION

How many *l*'s and *p*'s are there in Phi ? i ? ines? How many *t*'s and *n*'s in Bri ? a ? ica? How many *r*'s and *s*'s in emba ? a ? ing? How many *l*'s in acce ? erate?

A good, natural speller is gifted with a photographic mind. He can recall the word in print and count the number of *r*'s, *n*'s, *s*'s, and *l*'s in a word.

But not all of us have this power of observation. We have a vague idea of what the word looks like. Besides, none of us could accurately photograph the thousands of words we need to know the spelling of. And yet we need to know how to spell. It is just as disgraceful to misspell as to make illiterate mistakes in usage and speech.

Fortunately, there are ways of improving our spelling. There are easy ways of getting ourselves to look at words more closely and more effectively. There are ways of improving our powers of observation. But before we go into that, try these paired sentences.

## DOES IT MAKE ANY DIFFERENCE TO YOU?

1. In which was the legendary bowman surprisingly careless?
   *a.* Robin Hood was about to loose his arrow.
   *b.* Robin Hood was about to lose his arrow.

2. In the days when primogeniture meant everything, which was the more likely expostulation of the eldest son?
   *a.* I was there first.
   *b.* I was their first.

3. Which sounds conspiratorial?
   *a.* We'd like to invite you to dessert with us tomorrow evening.
   *b.* We'd like to invite you to desert with us tomorrow evening.

4. Which draft board's needs were the greatest?
   *a.* The medical board accepted men with perforated eardrums.
   *b.* The medical board excepted men with perforated eardrums.

5. Which statement is concerned with ethical standards?
   *a.* The principles in the case are well known.
   *b.* The principals in the case are well known.

6. Which Joe is the eager beaver?
   *a.* Joe submitted to many orders.
   *b.* Joe submitted too many orders.

7. Which question would an investigator ask about a specific group?
   *a.* Were there voices raised in protest?
   *b.* Were their voices raised in protest?

8. Which sounds like the title of an ode by Keats, Shelley, or Wordsworth?
   *a.* Too Early Spring.
   *b.* To Early Spring.

9. In which case are the chains not firmly fixed?
   *a.* You have nothing too loose but your chains.
   *b.* You have nothing to lose but your chains.

10. Which headline reveals a scandalous situation?

    a. SALE OF NARCOTICS IN HOSPITAL BARRED    b. SALE OF NARCOTICS IN HOSPITAL BARED

## 1. THE ARCHITECTURAL APPROACH

If we look closely at words, we shall find that most words are not one word but often two or three or four words put together—or parts of words that we see over and over again in other words. If we look closely at words we shall see that there are family relationships and resemblances. *Imagination* and *imaginative* are descendants of *image,* the parent word. *Accelerate* and *celerity* are first cousins, certainly. *Definitely, finish, finite,* and *infinity* are not strangers. Notice what we've accomplished already. We are not likely to put two *m*'s in *imagination* if we know it comes from *image.* We won't spell it *definately* if we know it's related to *finish* and *finite.* So, first, we must observe relationships of words.

This will become easier if we become architects and wreckers, if we build words up and then knock them down again. *Unbusinesslike* and *unimaginative* are good words to begin with. They're easy to break down.

un busy ness like

(We'll find out later why the *y* changes to *i.*)

un imag(e) in(e) ative

(We'll find out later why the *e*'s are dropped)

If we do it with other words we see hidden relationships:

pre par ation
se par ation

and we know that *separate* is not spelled *sep(e)rate.*

When we are able to see words in all their parts, see the bricks that put them together, we are well on the road to becoming intelligent—not hit-or-miss—spellers.

The bricks with which we build words are of three kinds. The central part of the word—the one that tells you what family it belongs to—is called the ROOT.

con sci ence
con sci ous

*Sci* is the root. The brick we place to the left of the root (or before it) is called the PREFIX. The brick we place to the right of the root (or after it) is called the SUFFIX. Notice that we can add another prefix and suffix to *conscious* and get *un con sci ous ly* or we can take a prefix away from *conscience* and get *science.* And now *conscience* and *conscious* should never give us any trouble. We've taken them apart, and we've seen what makes them tick.

Using this process, see how quickly spelling demons are tamed and spelling mysteries solved.

| | | | |
|---|---|---|---|
| rep ? tition | *e* or *i*? | Clue word—*petition* | Solved |
| reco ? endation | one *m* or two? | Clue word—*commend* | Solved |
| hum ? rous | *e* or *o*? | Clue word—*humor* | Solved |
| caf ? teria | *a, i,* or *e*? | Clue word—*cafe* | Solved |
| exhil ? rate | *e, a,* or *o*? | Clue word—*hilarious* | Solved |
| incrim ? nate | *a, e,* or *i*? | Clue word—*criminal* | Solved |
| i ? idescent | one *r* or two? | Clue word—*iris* | Solved |

## 2. THE MATHEMATICAL APPROACH

To the building and wrecking process we're going to apply a little simple arithmetic. We're going to add the last letter of the prefix and the first letter of the word to which it is attached.

Let's take words beginning with *dis* as an example:

dis + appoint (1 + 0 = 1 s)
dis + sect (1 + 1 = 2 s's)

(By the way there is no such word as *disect*. The word is either *dis* + *sect,* to cut up into many pieces, or *bi* + *sect*, to cut in two.)

Now try these and decide by arithmetic whether there should be one *s* or two.

1. di (ss) olve, 2. di (ss) ervice, 3. di (ss) appear, 4. di (ss) ent, 5. di (ss) illusioned, 6. di (ss) array, 7. di (ss) ident, 8. di (ss) ability, 9. di (ss) integrate, 10. di (ss) agree, 11. di (ss) imilar, 12. di (ss) approve, 13. di (ss) atisfied, 14. di (ss) assemble, 15. di (ss) unity, 16. di (ss) uade, 17. di (ss) engage, 18. di (ss) onance, 19. mi (ss) pell, 20. mi (ss) appropriate.

Did you notice that if a recognizable word appeared after (ss), there was only one *s?* Why?

Now we'll look at the end of the word and add the first letter of the suffix and the last of the central word.

### The Suffix **ly**

accidental + ly  Problem: one *l* or two?
Solution: 1 + 1 = 2
usual + ly  Problem: one *l* or two?
Solution: 1 + 1 = 2

Try the suffix *ness* yourself:

mean + ness  Problem: one *n* or two?
stubborn + ness  Problem: one *n* or two?

Some of the dragons have been slain. *Disappoint* is easy now. It has only one *s*. Why? Because $1 + 0 = 1$. No more trouble from *especially*. $1 + 1 = 2$.

It is easy to see now that when a prefix ends in a vowel (re, pro) it will be followed by a single, not a doubled, consonant ($0 + 1 = 1$). That settles *professional* and *recommend*.

Do some word building and wrecking on your own. Just to make sure you develop a PRE and SUF FIXation, here are a variety of prefixes and suffixes. Notice especially how the $1 + 1$ and $1 + 0$ rule operates.

| | |
|---|---|
| sym metrical | cor respond |
| ir responsible | com mission |
| un necessary | dis illusioned |
| in oculate | dis solution |
| il legible | drunken ness |
| im migration | practical ly |
| ab origines | beautiful ly |
| ab breviate | usual ly |

## 3. SPELLING BY EAR

So far we have stopped to look at the word to see what it is made of. Now we're going to listen—to listen *before* and *after* we spell a word.

The following misspellings are all due to slovenly pronunciations:

| | |
|---|---|
| goverment *for* government | heighth *for* height |
| libary *for* library | preform *for* perform |
| congradulations *for* congratulations | umberella *for* umbrella |
| pronounciation *for* pronunciation | suprise *for* surprise |
| athaletics *for* athletics | reconize *for* recognize |
| lenth *for* length | hinderance *for* hindrance |

The following misspellings would never occur if you tried to pronounce the words after writing them:

| | |
|---|---|
| villiage *for* village | tradegy *for* tragedy |
| similiar *for* similar | villian *for* villain |
| barbarious *for* barbarous | intergrate *for* integrate |
| captian *for* captain | mischievious *for* mischievous |

You cannot spell some words correctly unless you pronounce them correctly! And when you have spelled a word you must be able, with the letters in the order in which you have written them, to pronounce it correctly.

If you spell *necessary* with two *c*'s, you will have to pronounce it *neksessary;* if you spell *occasion* with two *s*'s it must rhyme with *passion.*

These are the big rules in spelling: STOP! LOOK! LISTEN!

1. Look at the word, see it in its component parts: build up a short word, break down a long word. Be observant. Become syllable-conscious. Get a *pre* and *suf fix*ation.

2. In adding prefixes and suffixes, also add the initial and final letters of the central word—$1 + 1 = 2$, $1 + 0 = 1$, $0 + 1 = 1$.

3. Listen to the sound of words. Pronounce them correctly before you spell them. Be able to pronounce them correctly after you spell them.

## WHICH VOWEL IS IT: A, E, I, O, or U?

Sometimes listening will not help you much, because vowels may lose their identity when they appear in an *unaccented* syllable. Words like *med ? cine* and *mir ? cle* present such a problem. Is it an *a*, *e*, *i*, *o*, *u*, or *y* where the question mark now appears? Your ear doesn't give you the answer.

Spell it med(a)cine, med(e)cine, med(i)cine, med(o)cine, or med(u)cine, and—if you hit the accented syllable *med* hard—all five will be pronounced exactly alike. For we are dealing with an indeterminate, neutral vowel sound that is now represented in all dictionaries by the symbol ə —known as the schwa. Therefore the words *medicine* and *miracle* appear in dictionaries as

měd'ə-sən and mĭr'ə-kəl

Because in our longer words there are more unaccented syllables than accented ones, the schwas probably outnumber all the other vowels put together. But that's nothing to cheer about, because to spell many of the words correctly, we must unmask the schwa and restore the vowel's identity.

How do we do this? By finding a related word in which the vowel in doubt (the schwa) appears in an *accented* syllable: for MEDicine the clue word would be meDICinal and for MIRacle the clue word would be mirACulous.

Don't let this explanation throw you. It's really very easy, as you will see when you come to do the exercise.

## THE SCHWA UNMASKED

(The first eight clue words have been supplied and the accented syllables indicated by capital letters. After that you are on your own.)

| VOWEL IN QUESTION | CLUE WORD | UNMASKED VOWEL |
|---|---|---|
| 1. aCAD ? my | acaDEMic | ? |
| 2. apPROXim ? tely | approxiMAtion | ? |
| 3. arisTOCr ? cy | aristoCRATic | ? |
| 4. aRITHm ? tic | arithMETical | ? |
| 5. AUth ? r | auTHORity | ? |
| 6. CENS ? r | cenSORious | ? |
| 7. CHA ? s | chaOTic | ? |
| 8. COLL ? ge | colLEgiate | ? |

* * *

9. comp ? TItion
10. conSERV ? tory
11. cor ? NAtion
12. CUSt ? dy
13. DEFin ? te
14. deMOCr ? cy
15. disCRIMin ? tory
16. disPENS ? ry
17. DOMin ? nce
18. DYn ? sty
19. d ? SPAIR
20. eCON ? my
21. EMph ? sis
22. exhil ? RAtion
23. exPLAN ? tory
24. ECst ? sy
25. FALl ? cy
26. FEL ? ny
27. FRIV ? lous
28. GRAMm ? r
29. horIZ ? n
35. inFLAMm ? tory
36. INflu ? nce
37. MAGn ? tism
38. MED ? cine
39. MIR ? cle
40. MOL ? cule
41. moNOT ? nous
42. NARr ? tive
43. NEUtr ? l
44. not ? RIety
45. NUm ? rous
46. NUtr ? tive
47. obSERV ? tory
48. paRAL ? sis
49. persp ? RAtion
50. PREV ? lent
51. PROD ? gy
52. reCIPr ? cate
53. reFORM ? tory
54. REL ? tive
55. REM ? dy

30. hyGI ? ne
31. hyPOCr ? sy
32. idioSYNcr ? sy
33. iMAGin ? tive
34. INfin ? te
56. repreSENT ? tive
57. RHAPs ? dy
58. SCHOL ? r
59. SPECt ? cle
60. SYN ? nym

## DANGEROUS CROSSING: **SILENT E**

When we cross over from a silent *e* to *ing* or *able* or any other suffix beginning with a vowel the *e* is dropped.

come—coming
write—writing
love—lovable
grieve—grievance
please—pleasant
serve—service
delegate—delegation
mortgage—mortgagor
prime—primal
fortune—fortunate
sense—sensible
futile—futility
store—storage
sterile—sterilize

Exception 1: Words ending in *ce* or *ge* keep the *e* before *able* and *ous* in order to retain the *s* and *j* sound.

*changeable, noticeable, courageous*

Exception 2: Some few words keep the *e* even before *ing* in order to retain their meaning clearly.

*singeing, dyeing, shoeing, hoeing, toeing*

Exception 3: *mileage*
Exception 4: Before *able* the *e* may be retained: *loveable, moveable, etc.*

When, however, we cross over to a suffix beginning with a consonant, the *e* does not drop out.

sincere—sincerely
care—careful
bore—boredom
immediate—immediately

Exceptions: *judgment, acknowledgment* (preferred in America), *wholly, duly, truly,* and *argument.*
Caution: Be sure to keep the *e* in words like *loneliness, likelihood, livelihood,* etc.

## DANGEROUS CROSSING: Y

When crossing over from a word ending in *y*, change the *y* to an *i* before all suffixes except *ing*.

try—tried
busy—business
lonely—loneliness
country—countries
marry—marriage
penny—penniless

BUT

*studying, hurrying, marrying*

Exception 1: Words ending in *ay, ey,* and *oy* do not change the *y* to *i*.

*valleys, monkeys, boyish*

Exception 2: *laid, paid, daily, gaily* (or *gayly*), *gaiety* (or *gayety*)

## DANGEROUS CROSSING: FINAL CONSONANTS

Watch the crossing carefully when there's a final consonant. An editor was once very much embarrassed when his newspaper in writing a laudatory column about one of the town's leading citizens called him a "battle-scared veteran." To make amends the editor wrote a correction for the next morning's edition. Unfortunately, the typesetter got there first with "a bottle-scarred veteran."

Words of *one* syllable that end in *one* consonant preceded by *one* vowel *double* the consonant before *ing, ed,* and *er*.

hop — hopped — hopping — hopper
plan — planned — planning — planner
bar — barred — barring
step — stepped — stepping — stepper
beg — begged — begging — beggar

When the word has more than one syllable, *listening* becomes our most important guide, for it is only when the accent falls *on the syllable containing the consonant* that we double the consonant. Notice how this rule works in the words given below:

reFER—reFERRing, but REFerence
preFER—preFERRing, but PREFerence and PREFerable
ocCUR—ocCURRing—ocCURRence
conTROL—conTROLLing—unconTROLLable
beGIN—beGINNing—beGINNer
eQUIP—eQUIPPed, but eQUIPment because the suffix does not begin with a vowel
comMIT—comMITTing—comMITTee, but comMITment

BUT

| | | |
|---|---|---|
| QUARrel | | QUARreling |
| TRAvel | | TRAveling |
| BENefit | | BENefiting |
| COLor | | COLoring |
| WORship | | WORshiping |
| MARvel | MARvelous | MARveling |

Exception: In England this rule is not strictly adhered to. You can usually recognize an English novel by its double *l* and double *p* spellings *(marvellous, travelling, worshipped).* We prefer streamlining and apply the rule rather strictly. Considering the many words involved, we have very few exceptions:

chagRINed, CANcellation (but CANceled), CRYStallize, METallurgy, HANdicapped, HANdicapper, and KIDnapper (with one or two p's).

## DANGEROUS CROSSINGS: MISCELLANEOUS

Words ending in *c* add a *k* before joining with *ed, ing,* or *y* in order to keep the hard sound of *c.*

picnicking, panicky, picnicker, shellacking

Verbs ending in *ie* usually drop the *e* and change the *i* to *y* before joining with *ing.*

*die—dying, tie—tying, lie—lying, vie—vying*

## OTHER PROBLEMS

Most of our other problems deal with the endings of words, all except the first one.

### IE or EI?

When the sound is *ee* and you don't know whether to use *ie* or *ei,* remember that *ei* follows the letter *c,* and *ie* all other letters.

*ceiling, receive, belief, chief, besiege*

Exceptions: *seize, weird, leisure, neither, sheik,* and *inveigle* (the last four words are not really exceptions since the *ei* is sometimes pronounced differently)

When any other sound is produced, use *ei.*

*foreign, forfeit, neighbor, height, heinous*

Exceptions: *sieve, handkerchief, mischief, mischievous* (the last three are really not exceptions since they are related to the word *chief*)

## ABLE or IBLE?

There is no very good rule, but here's a homemade one that works for many words. When you can form a word ending in *ation,* ABLE should be used. When you can form a word ending in *ion, tion, id,* or *ive,* IBLE is usually correct.

### ABLE WORDS

| | |
|---|---|
| indispensable (dispensation) | execrable (execration) |
| commendable (commendation) | excitable (excitation) |
| estimable (estimation) | irritable (irritation) |
| durable (duration) | inviolable (violation) |

### IBLE WORDS

| | |
|---|---|
| accessible (accession) | digestible (digestive) |
| audible (audition) | indefensible (defensive) |
| collectible (collection) | irrepressible (repressive) |
| comprehensible (comprehensive) | irresistible (resistive) |
| convertible (conversion) | suggestible (suggestive) |

## CEED, CEDE, or SEDE?

Only three words end in *ceed: exceed, proceed,* and *succeed.* Only one word ends in *sede: supersede.* All other words end in *cede: accede, intercede, precede,* etc.

## CE or SE?

In general, where the noun and verb are similar the noun ends in *ce,* the verb in *se.*

advice—advise    device—devise    prophecy—prophesy

We spell *license, defense,* and *pretense* with *se* but the English prefer *ce.* The word *suspense,* however, can be spelled only with an *se.*

## ER, RE?

British spelling prefers *re* in words that we spell *er* as in *theater, center, maneuver, caliber,* etc. In order to keep the hard sound of *c* and *g* we use *re* in *ogre, acre, massacre,* and *mediocre,* but not in *eager* and *meager.*

## OR, OUR?

In America, true to the principle of streamlining, we choose *or* when confronted with a choice of *or* or *our.* The only word we honor (not honour) with the *our* spelling is *glamour* (but glamorous).

## OUS or US?

Nouns end in *us,* adjectives in *ous.*
Nouns: *callus, mucus, phosphorus, fungus*
Adjectives: *callous, mucous,* etc.

## OS or OES?

Words that end in *o* give difficulty when the plurals are formed. (They should give no trouble in the singular, though there are those who like to put an *e* on *potato* and *hero.*) The best way to look at this problem is to say that the usual way to form the plural is to add *es* and call all the others exceptions.

Exception 1: Words ending in *io* or *eo* add only *s*: *cameos, ratios, studios.*

Exception 2: Words that are musical terms add only *s*: *sopranos, altos, oratorios, virtuosos.*

Exception 3: Words that are clipped forms add only *s*: *photos, curios, dynamos.*

Exception 4: Words recently adopted add only *s*: *commandos, gauchos, generalissimos.*

## WORDS SOMETIMES CONFUSED

Here, too, the right pronunciation will help.

accept, except (see page 86)
affect, effect (see page 86)
angle, angel—an *angle* is a part of a triangle, an *angel* isn't.
coarse, course—*coarse* is opposite of fine or refined.
cite, site, sight—*cite* (v) means quote; *site* (n) means place.
canvas, canvass—to *canvass* means to solicit or seek orders.
capital, capitol (see page 91)
complement, compliment—*complement* is related to complete.
consul, council, counsel
desert (v), desert (n), dessert (n)—*dessert* is the sweet course.
human, humane—*humane* means kind.
its, it's—*it's* equals *it is*, sometimes *it has*.
later, latter—*later* is opposite of earlier.
lose, loose—*loose* is opposite of tight.
moral, morale—the *morale* of a people is its capacity to take it.
past, passed—*passed* is the *past* of pass.
principal, principle (see page 103)
quiet (adj), quite (adv)—*quiet* is still.
stationary (adj), stationery (n)—we write on *stationery*.
than, then—then answers the question "when?"
their, they're, there—*they're* equals *they are; their* means belonging to them.
to, too, two—*too* means *too* much or also.
weather, whether—we talk about the *weather*.
who's, whose—*who's* means *who is*.

## I

## SPELLING: SILENT E AND FINAL CONSONANTS

If *ing* were added to each of the following words, would the word have a doubled consonant?

| A | B |
|---|---|
| 1. sin | 1. compel |
| 2. bar | 2. permit |
| 3. stoop | 3. signal |
| 4. din | 4. unwrap |
| 5. bat | 5. credit |
| 6. hope | 6. linger |
| 7. scrap | 7. allot |
| 8. dine | 8. outwit |
| 9. hug | 9. profit |
| 10. dot | 10. forget |
| 11. ship | 11. differ |
| 12. sun | 12. confer |
| 13. lag | 13. counsel |
| 14. shine | 14. overstep |
| 15. write | 15. travel |

## II

## SPELLING: EI AND IE

Copy each of the following words, inserting either *ei* or *ie* in the blank space.

| | |
|---|---|
| 1. y——ld | 6. s——smic |
| 2. bel——ve | 7. rec——pt |
| 3. bes——ge | 8. ch——ftain |
| 4. unw——ldy | 9. sover——gn |
| 5. dec——ve | 10. s——zure |

## III

Rewrite the following sentences, filling each of the blanks with one of the words that appears in parentheses.

1. . . . are good reasons why . . . about to sell . . . house. *(there, their, they're)*

2. . . . not . . . late . . . give the cat . . . milk. *(its, it's, to, too)*

3. If . . . going home, take . . . books with you. *(your, you're)*

4. Do you know . . . the . . . is pleasant there? *(weather, whether)*

5. They . . . known for a long time that you would . . . gone if you had heard . . . the game in time. *(nave, of, 've)*

6. Where . . . are many opinions, most people feel . . . justified in holding on to . . . own; and while . . . several scientific explanations for this stubbornness, . . . be few changes unless we can convince men that they ought to be more open-minded. *(there, their, they're, there're, there'll)*

7. My . . . objection to the . . . of that school is that he is a man of no . . . *(principal, principle)*

8. Not until . . . will you be able to tell whether you have more . . . you need. *(than, then)*

9. If your strap is . . . , you may . . . your books. *(lose, loose)*

10. Not even in the . . . would I . . . the table before . . . . *(desert, dessert)*

11. ". . . going to punch . . . nose?" demanded Jerry belligerently. *(whose, who's)*

## IV

## SPELLING DEMONS

In each of the following groups, one of the words is misspelled. In each case spell correctly the misspelled word.

1. already, altogether, alright, always
2. publicity, accidently, essentially, legibly
3. absence, license, suspence, defense
4. disease, agreement, buisness, bicycle
5. accumulate, surround, accomodate, collaborate
6. biscuit, consious, vicious, spacious

7. sacrafice, obstacle, realistic, miracle
8. friend, decided, resistence, anoint
9. dining room, trapped, comming, stopped
10. recomend, accurately, committee, interrupt
11. dissatisfied, dissappoint, disappearance, misspelled
12. quantities, grammer, beggar, calendar
13. cafeteria, adequate, mathamatics, medicine
14. illegible, eligible, oblige, privelege
15. posesses, assistant, harass, balance
16. cemetery, referee, seperate, inoculate
17. ninth, sincerly, jewelry, truly
18. library, balloon, suprise, February
19. acheivement, ceiling, foreign, siege
20. suddenness, succeed, until, accross
21. shriek, beleive, seize, chief
22. controlled, begining, quarreling, allotted
23. amount, aviator, opinion, vallies
24. origin, conqueror, auther, whether
25. pleasant, beautiful, repitition, enemies
26. tradgedy, cavalry, recognize, perform
27. persuading, conscience, persuing, finally
28. attacked, ammunition, artillery, writting
29. coolly, disected, meanness, innocent
30. couragous, judgment, noticeable, valuable
31. pronunciation, bachelor, charachter, children
32. enviorment, strength, government, temperature
33. descendants, discipline, dissolve, discription
34. envelope, elaborate, servicable, ninety
35. independence, existance, attendance, convenience
36. humerous, mysterious, barbarous, courtesy
37. imaginary, immitate, immature, immigration
38. personally, scarcely, immediatly, really
39. beautiful, especially, continually, definately
40. arctic, bookkeeping, neccessary, escape
41. predjudice, college, etc., colossal
42. conquering, occassionally, parallel, incidentally
43. familiar, occurence, equipped, omitted
44. changeable, livelihood, lonliness, desirable
45. casualities, similar, athletics, umbrella
46. chocolate, banana, commitment, stomache
47. opportunity, murmer, burglar, nickel

48. concensus, countries, refugees, exercise
49. village, captain, villian, lieutenant
50. assassin, embarrass, career, dessicated

## SPELLING BONERS

Here are some boners (usually connected with books students studied and were required to write about) that I have collected over the years. They are choice in the sense that they make sense anyhow and fit amusingly into the context of the sentence. Wherever it is a book that is discussed, the title is indicated. Correct the spelling of the crucial word.

1. Israel Hand tried to kill Jim Hawkins with a cutlet. *(Treasure Island)*

2. Beret was a religious woman, and the customs and morality of the New World prayed on her mind. *(Giants in the Earth)*

3. Here Charles Lindbergh tells the story of his long months of planing before his epic flight. *(The Spirit of St. Louis)*

4. At the end of Edith Wharton's tragic story, Ethan and Mattie, seeing no other way out, decide to go on a slay ride. *(Ethan Frome)*

5. Godfrey Cass was the kind of person who gets angry slowly but surly. *(Silas Marner)*

6. By nightfall David had walked only an infinidecimal part of the way to his aunt's house. *(David Copperfield)*

7. Just by looking at Osric, as he fanned himself with his hat, you could tell he was self-scented. *(Hamlet)*

8. Everyone thought that she was a sweet, lovely child but she had killing in her blood—she was a congenial murderer. *(The Bad Seed)*

9. Charles Lamb's "Dissipation on Roast Pig" is the kind of literature that helps one to relax.

10. Count Vronsky was a very good-looking man and had courted many women without ever marring them. *(Anna Karenina)*

11. What he enjoyed most was the power he wheeled over his students. *(Good-bye, Mr. Chips)*

12. He was so popular he was elected anonymously.

13. He was so famished, he just gouged himself.

14. Ibsen's *A Doll's House* teaches a lesson to people who are married and even to those who are singular.

15. At the climax of the play, Nora, realizing that she has been playing a doll for a husband who has been interested only in himself, says angrily, "Now the masterade is over." *(A Doll's House)*

## CAPITAL OR SMALL LETTERS?

The purpose of beginning a word with a capital letter is to give the word proper prominence or to pay it due respect. Here are a few reminders.

1. Capitalize the names of peoples, their languages, and their religions.

> English, Chinese, Negro, Indian, American, Christian, Buddhist

2. Capitalize street, bank, professor, governor, war, high school, river, county *only* when they are used with names that designate them as specific places or persons.

> Fifth Avenue, First National Bank, Professor Boas, the Civil War, New York University

*a.* The word President when it means the President of the United States, even though the name is not used.
*b.* The South only when it specifically means the southern states.
*c.* Don't capitalize spring, summer, fall or winter.

3. Titles of books, articles, magazines, newspapers, and songs. Capitalize the first word and all others except articles and short prepositions and conjunctions.

Henrik Ibsen's *An Enemy of the People*

4. In a letter only the first and last words of the salutation and only the first word of the complimentary close.

My dear Sir:
Yours very sincerely,

5. All adjectives derived from proper nouns begin with capitals.

French fries, Danish cheeses, Polish hams, American know-how, British actors, Italian films

6. We capitalize the names of all religions and of the deity and all pronouns referring to Him (except *who*, though there is divided usage here).

God, Lord, the Almighty, the Creator

However, the word *god* is not capitalized when referring to the gods of mythology, but the names of individual gods and goddesses are: Athena, Juno, Zeus, Thor, Isis.

7. The names of sacred books are capitalized *without quotation marks*.

the Bible, the New Testament, the Koran, the Talmud

8. In relationships—out of respect to the person addressed or referred to—we use capitals.

Please, Mother, I want to do it myself.

or

I called Mother last night.

but

I called my mother last night. (The word *my* seems to take the place of the capital letter.)

## EXERCISE ON USE OF CAPITAL LETTERS

Rewrite the passages below correctly, deciding whether the italicized words should begin with a capital letter:

> The *president*—with the approval of the *senate*—sent a *commission* to the *west* last *summer* to study the *customs* and *history* of the *indians* living on *government reservations.* The commission, which consisted of two *republicans* and three *democrats,* was headed by *captain* Olaf Jorgensen, who lives on *seventy-second street* in this *city.*
>
> The *captain* is of *norwegian ancestry* and is an honor *alumnus* of this *high school.* When he was a *senior,* he was *president* of the *g.o.* and a member of the *chess club.* At *commencement* he won awards in *english, mathematics,* and *social studies.* He went on to *michigan state university,* where he specialized in *sociology,* and where he was elected to *phi beta kappa* in his *junior* year. After spending two years as a pilot in *world war II,* he went to a *university* to complete work on his *ph.d.*
>
> The *captain's* report, which he intends to call *"an inquiry into the customs and history of the american indian,"* should be of great value to the *secretary of the interior* when he goes before the interested *congressional committees* to urge them to formulate the necessary *legislation.*

## SPELLING BEES

Long popular in America, the old-fashioned spelling bee has for many years, with the help of the microphone, been an annual contest.

If you are going to be a contestant in a spelling bee, here's a good list to study. If you are going to stage a spelling bee, here's your ammunition. Make sure the spelling master knows how to pronounce the words correctly.

## Light

400 words in constant use sometimes misspelled by you and me. Some of these may be too easy to use in a spelling bee, but will serve to limber up one's vowels and consonants. The easier words are printed in italics.

| | | | |
|---|---|---|---|
| *absence* | *arrival* | carriage | *conquer* |
| *accept* | *article* | *carrying* | conscience |
| *accident* | association | ceiling | conscious |
| accurately | *athletic* | celebrity | considerable |
| achievement | *attacked* | *certain* | continually |
| across | attendance | changeable | controlled |
| *address* | author | *changing* | convenience |
| adequate | audience | chaos | *corner* |
| *advice* | aviator | character | *council* (group) |
| agreement | *awkward* | *chief* | *countries* |
| | | | |
| *airplane* | balance | *children* | *consul* |
| aisle (theater) | beautiful | chocolate | courageous |
| allege | *because* | *choose* | *course* (n) |
| all right | *before* | *chosen* | *courteous* |
| *almost* | beggar | *climbed* | courtesy |
| *already* | beginning | *clothes* | *crowd* |
| *altogether* | believed | *cloud* | crucial |
| amateur | bicycle | *coarse* (not fine) | deceive |
| *among* | *brakes* (car) | collar | *decided* |
| amount | *break* | college | decisively |
| | | | |
| *annual* | *breathe* | colonel | definite |
| *answer* | buried | *color* | dependent |
| *anxious* | business | *coming* | descendant |
| appearance | cafeteria | committee | description |
| appreciate | candidate | *common* | desirable |
| approaching | capitol | competition | despair |
| argument | (building) | completely | desperate |
| *around* | captain | compliment | dessert (sweets) |
| *aroused* | career | *conceal* | *destroy* |
| arrangements | *careful* | *confident* | *determine* |

develop
*device*
*dictator*
*didn't*
*different*
*dining room*
disappeared
disappointed
*discussed*
disease

dissatisfied
*divided*
*doctor*
*doesn't*
*dropped*
*dying*
*easily*
*effect* (result)
efficiency
*eighth*

eligible
*eminent*
enemies
emphasize
*English*
*entirely*
environment
equipped
especially
essentially

*etc.*
*everybody*
exceed
*excellent*
exercise
excitement
exhausted
existence
*expense*
*experience*

explanation
*extremely*
familiar
fascinating
*fatigue*
*February*
finally
financial
forcibly
foreign

foresee
*formerly* (time)
*forth* (ahead)
forty
*fourteen*
*fourth*
*friend*
*fugitive*

*future*
*generally*
*genius*
*government*
grammar
grievance
guarantee
*guard*
*handle*
*handful*

*handsome* (adj)
harassed
*hasn't*
*height*
*hoping*
humorous
*hundred*
*hungry*
*hurriedly*

*hurrying*
identity
imaginary
immediately
indefinitely
independence
influential
*instead*
integrate
interfere

interrupt
*invitation*
*its* (possessive)
*jealous*
jewelry
*judgment*
*knowledge*
*ladies*
*laid*
*latter*

*led* (v)
legible
lieutenant
*library*
lightning (flash)
literature
livelihood
loneliness
*loose*
*losing*

loveliness
*lying*
*magazine*
marriage
meanness
*meant*
medicine
*merely*
*minutes*
miracle

misspelled
mournful
*movable*
murmur
muscle
mysterious
naturally
necessary
*neither*
*nevertheless*

*nickel*
*niece*
*ninety*
ninth
noticeable
oblige
obstacle
occasion
occurred
*o'clock*

*officer*
omitted
*operate*
opinion
opportunity
organization
origin
*paid*
particular
*partner*

*passed* (v)
pastime
*perform*
*perhaps*
*permanent*
personally
persuading
physically
*piece* (fragment)

*planning*
pleasant
*politics*
portrayed
possesses
*possible*
practically
preceding
preference
preferred

prejudice
preparations
*presence*
principal (chief)
principles
(rules)
privilege
*probably*
proceeded
professional

professor
*prominent*
*proved*
pursuing
quantities
quarreling
*quarter*
*quiet* (still)
*quizzes*
*realize*
*really*
*receipt*

*received*
*recognize*
recommend
referee
reference
referred
refugee
relieve
religious
remedy

repetition
representative
requirements
resistance
resources
respectability
restaurant
rhyme
sacrifice
*safety*

*sandwich*
*Saturday*
*scarcely*
scene
schedule
*secretary*
seize
*sentence*
separate
sergeant
severely
*shining*

*shriek*
siege
similar
sincerely
specimen
*speech*
stationary
(fixed)
stomach
*stopped*

*stories*
*straight* (direct)
*strength*
*stretched*
*strictly*
*striking*
*studying*
*succeed*
suddenness
*summer*

*surely*
surprise
*surround*
suspense
technical
temperature
tendency
*their* (poss.)
*those*
*threw*
tobacco
*together*

*too* (too cold)
*toward*
tragedy
transferred
*tries*
*truly*
*twelfth*
*until*
*unusual*
*useful*

usually
valleys
valuable
*varied*
vegetable
village
villain
*wasn't*
*weather*
Wednesday

*weird*
*welfare*
whether
(or not)
*which*
*whose* (poss.)
woman (one)
*women* (many)
*wonderful*
*wouldn't*
writing
*written*

## Medium

350 words often used, many of which will knock out the run-of-the-mill spelling experts.

| | | | |
|---|---|---|---|
| abscess | apparatus | boycott | contemptibly |
| abysmal | apparent | brilliancy | convalescent |
| academy | appeasement | bulletin | coolly |
| accessible | appetite | buoyancy | corporal |
| accidentally | appropriately | burglar | corpuscle |
| accommodate | approximately | calendar (dates) | correspondence |
| accumulate | architecture | camphor | corridor |
| acknowledge | artillery | casualties | corroborate |
| acquaintance | assassination | catastrophe | counterfeit |
| acquiescent | assessment | cavalry | criticism |
| | | | |
| acquisition | assimilate | cemetery | crocheting |
| acquittal | astronaut | charisma | cruiser |
| advantageous | asylum | chauffeur | crystallize |
| affidavit | auspicious | clientele | cylindrical |
| affiliated | bachelor | coincidence | deficiency |
| aggressor | banana | collaborator | delineation |
| agreeably | bandage | collateral | development |
| allegiance | bankruptcy | colossal | digestible |
| allotted | barbarous | column | dilemma |
| almanac | bargain | communiqué | diphtheria |
| | | | |
| ambassador | battalion | comparatively | disastrous |
| ambiguity | beleaguered | compelling | discernible |
| ammunition | belligerent | competent | disciplinary |
| analysis | beneficiary | compulsory | discriminatory |
| annihilation | benefited | concentration | dissection |
| anniversary | bigoted | conciliatory | disseminate |
| anoint | biscuit | conqueror | dissertation |
| anonymous | blasphemous | conscientiously | dissipation |
| anticipate | bookkeeper | consensus | drunkenness |
| apologetically | bourgeois | contagious | dynamic |

eccentricity
ecology
ecstasy
effervescent
elimination
elucidate
embarrassment
emigrate
emphasize
encyclopedia

enigma
enthusiastically
epitome
erratic
erroneous
espionage
etiquette
exaggerate
exhibition
exhilarated

exonerate
extraordinarily
extravagance
facetiously
facilities
fascism
felicitating
feminine
fictitious
fiery

foreboding
forfeit
fundamentally
furlough
gelatin
goddess
granary
grievous
guerrilla (also one r)

guillotine
gymnasium
helicopter
hindrance
hygiene
hypnotism
hypocrisy
hypothesis
illegible
illiterate

imitation
immigration
imminent
impair
inaccuracy
incessant
incidentally
indispensable
inevitable
inexhaustible

inexorable
inflammable
ingenious (clever)
ingenuous (naïve)
inimitable
innocence
innumerable
insistence

insurrection
intellectual
intelligence
intercede
intimacy
intricacy
irascible
irrelevant
irreparable
irretrievable

irritable
isolationist
jocose
khaki
laboratory
lavender
legitimate
likelihood
liquefy
macaroni

macaroons
mahogany
maintenance
maneuver
massacre
materiel (military)
mathematics
mechanically
medieval

mediocre
melancholy
millionaire
miniature
mischievous
miscellaneous
molasses
momentous
monastery
monopoly

monotonous
mortgage
mucilage
naïve
narrative
nauseous
negligence
neuralgia
obedience
obituary

obstreperous
occasionally
occurrence
ominous
onerous
optimistic
orchestration
pantomime
parachute
parallel

paralysis
parliamentary
particularly
pasteurized
pavilion
perilous
permissible
perseverance
persistence
personnel

perspiration
pessimistic
phenomenon
Philippines
physician
physiological
picnicking
picturesque
pinnacle
plebiscite

plenipotentiary
poisonous
pollution
posthumous
pneumonia
prairie
precipice
predominant
prevalent
primitive

procedure
pronunciation
propaganda
prophecy
propeller
propitious
psychological
questionnaire
receptacle
recipe
reconnoiter
  (also *tre*)
recuperate
reinforcements
renowned
repetitious
rescind
reservoir
resiliency
reveille
rheumatism
rhythm
salient
satellite
scissors
scurrilous
serviceable
shepherd
silhouette
singeing
simultaneously
solicitous
sophomore
sophisticated
specifically
spontaneous
statistician
strategy
strenuous
subsistence
successfully
superfluous
supersede
superintendent
superstitious
supremacy
surgeon
surreptitious
surveillance
syllable
symbolic
symmetrical
symptomatic
synonym
tariff
tenant
thousandth
torpedoed
tortoise
totalitarian
tourniquet
treachery
tuberculosis
tyrannically
unaccustomed
unanimous
undoubtedly
unforgettable
unnecessarily
unprecedented
vacuum
vengeance
ventilation
wholly
wiry

## Heavy Artillery A

100 words occasionally used and guaranteed to knock out almost any speller.

abeyance
accelerator
accolade
aeronautics
amethyst
antediluvian
archipelago
asphyxiated
bailiwick
bouillon (broth)
boutonniere
broccoli
catarrhal
cenotaph
chameleon
chrysanthemum
cinnamon
connoisseur
diaphanous
dyspepsia
ecclesiastical
eczema
ellipsis
ephemeral
escutcheon
esophagus
feasibility
fricassee
genealogy
gherkin
hemorrhage
hieroglyphics
hippopotamus
homogeneous
hydrangeas
hypochondriac
idiosyncrasies
impecuniosity
impresario
innuendo
inoculate
iridescent
irresistibly
jeopardy
jodhpurs
kaleidoscopic
kimono
laryngitis
malleable
mayonnaise
metallurgical
metamorphosis
millennium
mineralogy
moccasin
neophyte

| | | | |
|---|---|---|---|
| neurasthenic | piccolo | rhinoceros | synonymous |
| obeisance | pomegranate | rhododendron | tattooist |
| omniscient | prescience | rhythmically | tobogganing |
| opprobrium | prophesied | saboteur | truculent |
| ordnance (army) | pseudonym | saccharine (adj) | ukulele |
| pachyderm | pyorrhea (or *rrhoea*) | sacrilegious | vacillation |
| panacea | rarefy | sarsaparilla | vermilion |
| paraffin | recalcitrant | saxophone | veterinarian |
| paroxysm | reconnaissance | soliloquies | vicissitude |
| paraphernalia | resuscitating | spaghetti | victuals |
| phosphorus (n) | ricocheting* | stereopticon | violoncello |
| | | | xylophone |

## Heavy Artillery B

50 words rarely used and wheeled out only for the knockout blow in the last round of a spelling bee.

| | | | |
|---|---|---|---|
| adscititious | caoutchouc | lackadaisical | pterodactyl |
| acetylene | centripetal | mausoleum | pusillanimous |
| agoraphobia | chrysoprase | miscegenation | ratiocination |
| amanuensis | cirrhosis | mnemonics | rococo |
| anemone | cloisonné | ocarina | schizophrenia |
| apocalypse | cuneiform | onomatopoeia | synecdoche |
| apocryphal | daguerreotype | overweening | syzygy |
| autochthonous | desiccate | pharmaceutical | thaumaturgist |
| baccalaureate | eleemosynary | philately | tintinnabulation |
| butyraceous | erysipelas | predaceous | triptych |
| cachinnation | euthanasia | prestidigitator | treglodyte |
| cacophony | hyperbole | psittacosis | |
| caffeine | isosceles | ptarmigan | |

* One *t* when pronounced ri-co-SHAY-ing; two *t's* when ri-co-SHET-*ting*.

Chapter 11

# Punctuation—Who Needs It?

## A COMPLETE GUIDE TO MODERN PUNCTUATION

### Punctuation Marks
### (Recognizing That Punctuation Marks Are Really the Traffic Signals of Clear Writing)

> All kinds of detailed comments and amendments have to be debated before the text can be adopted. It, in fact, took ten months to agree on every word and every comma (and members here will know that punctuation is almost as important as language in a document of this kind).
>
> —From a speech made in Geneva on December 1, 1960, before the First Committee of the United Nations by Mr. Ormsby-Gore, then Minister of State of the United Kingdom.

As if to prove the truth of what Mr. Ormsby-Gore said about the importance of punctuation, the three headlines printed below appeared in *The New York Times* between the years 1963 and 1965.

COMMA LEGALIZES SLAVERY

MISPLACED COMMA PUTS
DE GAULLE OUT OF FOCUS

FOR WANT OF HYPHEN
VENUS ROCKET IS LOST

## PUNCTUATION AS AN AID TO INSTANT CLARITY

Try this series of sentences. You will discover a good reason for giving attention to punctuation. Read the following ten sentences quickly. Just read them—nothing more.

1. If you wish to shoot the attendant will load the gun for you.

2. For some time after Philip was brokenhearted.

3. In the middle of a performance we saw Danny Kaye suddenly spied a six-year-old girl in the audience.

4. While we were eating the dog began to bark.

5. To write a history of the past ten years of research is a minimum requirement.

6. Two years before World War I had begun.

7. On the path leading to the cellar steps were heard.

8. I ran quickly for the bus was about to start.

9. Our team still has to play Lincoln and Madison must play Central High School.

10. Without the warm affection Bert felt in Uncle William's family life in Oregon was hard.

Did you understand the intent of these sentences at first sight? Or did you have to read some or all of them a second or third time to be sure of their meaning? Obviously something is missing in each sentence—some signal to warn the reader to slow down. Go back now and put in the slow-down commas which make the sentences *instantly* clear!

Now you ought to be able to answer the question that the chapter title asks: Punctuation: Who Needs It? The answer is obvious. The *reader* does.

## TRAFFIC SIGNS AND SIGNALS

Marks of punctuation are the traffic signs and signals that act as guides for the reader. They tell him where to STOP or SLOW DOWN; they tell him where the writer has taken a DETOUR or a SHORTCUT. Marks of punctuation prevent collisions among words. They make reading safer and surer. The following chart shows how certain punctuation marks are related to traffic signs:

| | |
|---|---|
| *The period* | . |
| *The question mark* | ? |
| *The exclamation point* | ! |

| | |
|---|---|
| *Quotation marks* | “ ” |
| *The period* | . |
| *The comma* | , |
| *Ellipses* | . . . |

| | |
|---|---|
| *The comma* | , |
| *The dash* | — |
| *The colon* | : |
| *The semicolon* | ; |

| | |
|---|---|
| *Commas in pairs* | , , |
| *Dashes in pairs* | — — |
| *Parentheses* | ( ) |
| *Brackets* | [ ] |

Punctuation marks are used in sentences for the same reason that traffic regulations and signs are used on the road:

1. To avoid collisions (between words);
2. To eliminate confusion (in meaning);
3. To point out the right direction (of the thought);
4. To indicate a detour (from the main thought);
5. To show that a shortcut has been taken.

And just as roads have become speed highways through the elimination of curves, the construction of overpasses, and the judicious placing of traffic signs, so today punctuation has also become streamlined. This is especially true of commas, which are used only where they'll do the most good.

## STOP SIGNS: THE PERIOD, THE QUESTION MARK, THE EXCLAMATION POINT

### The Period

1. Which expresses greater regret?
   *a.* I'm sorry. You can't come with us.
   *b.* I'm sorry you can't come with us.

2. Which sign would be better on (or over) a receptacle for litter?
   *a.* You can help. Throw it here.
   *b.* You can help throw it here.

3. Which is the incomplete job?
   *a.* That's all. I've finished.
   *b.* That's all I've finished.

Everyone knows that a period (the British call it a "full stop") comes at the end of a sentence. The only catch is that many don't know when to stop, don't know when one sentence ends and another begins. They are like careless drivers who slow down but do not come to a full stop at a stop sign. In writing, such carelessness results in the error variously referred to as a run-on sentence or a comma splice—joining two sentences with a comma instead of separating them with a period. Let's look at the following:

> Our team was lucky to win the game, with only seconds left to play Jones ran seventy yards to a touchdown.

A careful reading will show that there are two sentences here and that a full-stop sign (a period), not a slow-down sign (a comma), is needed between *game* and *with*.

Listed below are sentence fragments (incomplete sentences), complete sentences, and run-on sentences (two or more sentences written carelessly as one). Copy the number of each sentence and after each write F, C, or RO, depending on whether the sentence is a fragment, a correct or complete sentence, or a run-on sentence.

1. Although I don't usually enjoy poetry, I like this poem very much.

2. Especially the part in which the fight between the captain and the pirates takes place.

3. I admire many of the characters in the book I have just read, although the novel as a whole did not appeal to me.

4. For example, Jim Hawkins who was a very brave young fellow.

5. She'll never go through with it.

6. Unless she has more courage than we give her credit for.

7. His fishing line was hopelessly tangled, all attempts to straighten it out were futile.

8. You go and see what he wants, I'll wait here for you.

9. Because I can't stand being treated as if I were a stranger.

10. I'll never go to his house again, I'm sick of watching television all day.

## Question Marks and Exclamation Points

Of course, the question mark and the exclamation point may also be used at the end of a sentence. If someone asks you what terminal mark to use with *I did it,* your proper answer should be, "I don't know. You'll have to tell me what the writer means by *I did it.*"

For example, which of the terminal marks would you use for each of the meanings given in parentheses below?

> I did it—(a simple admission or confession)
> I did it—(a denial with strong doubt of the other person's sanity implied)
> I did it—(the greatest achievement since Edison's invention of the electric light)

Obviously, a question mark or an exclamation point at the end of a sentence is more expressive and says more than a period. For example, there's the story told about Victor Hugo, who, shortly after the appearance of *Les Misérables* in the bookshops, carried on the shortest correspondence on record—if we are to believe the story.

Hugo's letter to his publisher contained only the following:

> ?

To which the reply was:

> !

Hugo was a happy man, for he thus knew that *Les Misérables* was selling surprisingly well.

In *The Medium Is the Massage,* by Marshall McLuhan and Quentin Fiore, appears this sentence: "The hydrogen bomb is history's exclamation point. It ends an age-long sentence of manifest violence."

Even youngsters know they can play tricks with punctuation marks. On a lake in the Adirondacks there appeared this sign:

PRIVATE
NO SWIMMING
ALLOWED

By judiciously placing one of each of the three terminal marks of punctuation, pranksters changed this warning against trespassing into a public invitation to use the lake.

Can you do it? Use one period, one question mark, and one exclamation point.

CAUTION

The question mark should be used only for such direct questions as:

> Are you leaving today?
>
> Why is the departure of the plane being held up?

It is not used if the question is an indirect one:

> He asked me whether I was leaving today.
>
> I asked why the departure of the plane was being held up.

We also do not use the question mark when we are merely making a request or when we expect no answer:

> May I congratulate you on your recent appointment. (No answer is expected.)

> Will you please let all your friends know about the meeting. (This is merely a request.)
>
> May we have your attention for a moment. (This, too, is merely a request.)

*Note:* Occasionally question marks and exclamation points are used *within* sentences, as in the following:

> Civil rights and the ballet—do they seem like strange companions?—clasped hands last night in a stirring new production at the City Center.
>
> Civil rights as the theme of a ballet—what a stirring combination they made!—proved again the inventiveness of the City Center.

## EXERCISE IN THE USE OF TERMINAL PUNCTUATION

Now you can try your hand at using the period, the question mark, and the exclamation point in the following prose adaptation of a poem by Robert Browning.

In the quoted material—for the present—place all punctuation marks inside the terminal or closing quotation marks. This practice will be more fully explained on pages 223–35, in the section dealing with quotation marks.

Copy the paragraphs on a separate sheet of paper, inserting the necessary end punctuation. You'll find that reading the passage aloud will help you to determine not only where sentences end and new ones begin but also what the nature of the terminal punctuation marks should be. Capitalize the first letter of new sentences.

### CLIVE

*(Adapted from Robert Browning's poem of the same name)*

When General Clive was a young man, he went to work as a clerk in India for the East India Company one evening he was honored by an invitation to play cards with a party of young army officers of the Queen a young captain whose name has never been told sat next to Clive as he passed the cards to Clive, the captain said, "Cut"

Clive rose and said quietly, "Have you discovered a new way to cut cards you kept back a card when you handed them to me you cheated"

The other officers immediately jumped to their feet, amazed that one of their number had been accused of cheating to settle the difficulty at once and to uphold the honor of the army, a duel was arranged with pistols at ten paces as a nervous Clive and the confident captain stood facing each other, Clive's pistol accidentally exploded missing the captain's head only by inches.

It was now the captain's privilege—according to the laws of dueling—to shoot at Clive from where he pleased he strode over to the young man deliberately and held the pistol to Clive's temple exclaiming, "What was that you said to me"

"Captain," replied Clive slowly and steadily, "before you gave me those cards you took one out of the pack you know you did you cheated" The captain lowered his hand and then raised it again as if to fire again his hand dropped and he finally shouted, "You have the devil and God on your side, and I can't fight the three of you I did cheat"

Then he rushed out of the room for a moment the officers remained speechless, being too stunned to do or say anything then recovering from their shock, one of them shouted, "Get after him he's disgraced the uniform he must be punished"

"Just a moment," Clive said blocking their way "you didn't think him a cheat a minute ago, did you yet he was just as much a cheat then you were willing to see me murdered did you try to find out whether my accusation was just no that man treated me more fairly than you have"

Clive looked about the room, and when he had made a mental note of those present, he concluded,

"If any one of you in this room ever breathes a word against the captain, I promise not to be as charitable to you as he was to me"

SHORTCUT

## The Period in Abbreviations

The period is one of the most obvious ways of taking a shortcut. In addressing mail or when writing a letter, we may write "Ave." instead of "Avenue," "St." instead of "Street," "Calif." instead of "California." We do this because often the space accommodates the abbreviations better. (Sometimes we do it because we don't want to hazard the spelling of Massachusetts or Connecticut.) The United States Post Office has standardized abbreviations for each of the states.

Don't carry abbreviations over to cities. Don't write Pgh. and have your reader or the postman try to guess whether it's Pittsburgh or Poughkeepsie. And don't abbreviate the names of streets or avenues. If you do, you'll probably have your letter returned to you.

Avoid homemade abbreviations of any kind in formal writing. Stick to those that have been standardized.

### SOME STANDARD ABBREVIATIONS

Here are some standard abbreviations in which periods are necessary:

55 B.C.

A.D. 1942 (the number of the year always precedes B.C. and generally follows A.D.)

U.S.A.

U.S.S.R.

Ave. and St. (when the names precede)

Mr., Mrs., Dr. (when names follow)

### RECOGNIZING ABBREVIATIONS

What do the following abbreviations stand for? Those starred often omit the period(s).

| | | |
|---|---|---|
| 1. No. | 8. P.S. | 15. Md. |
| 2. cc.* | 9. Jr. | 16. P.T.A.* |
| 3. Hon. | 10. Ph.D. | 17. Va. |
| 4. C.O. | 11. M.A. | 18. V.A. |
| 5. Sr. | 12. A.M. | 19. R.S.V.P. |
| 6. R.N. | 13. P.M. | 20. c.o.d. |
| 7. vs. | 14. M.D. | 21. R.F.D.* |

Here are some Latin abbreviations, many of which you will come across frequently, especially in footnotes, when doing research.

| | |
|---|---|
| 1. i.e. | 6. et seq. |
| 2. c. or ca. | 7. ib., ibid. |
| 3. cf. | 8. op. cit. |
| 4. e.g. | 9. q.v. |
| 5. et al. | 10. viz. |

### ABBREVIATIONS WITHOUT PERIODS

The tendency to use capitals without periods is strong. No periods are used for call letters of radio or TV stations or for such points of the compass as SSW, SW (unless S.W. is a section of a city, as in London S.W. 1).

There is also a definite tendency to omit periods altogether in abbreviations of recent origin: NASA, NATO, SEATO, SAC, ESP.

As a matter of fact, in recent years organizations (governmental and otherwise) have tried to find a succession of capitals that form not only an easily pronounceable word but one that is meaningful and descriptive:

ZIP Code stands for Zone Improvement Plan and gives promise of speedier mail deliveries.

CARE stands for Cooperative for American Relief Everywhere and is self-explanatory.

PLATO stands for Programed Logic for Automatic Teaching Operation and, as every schoolboy knows, Plato was Socrates' pupil and Aristotle's teacher.

Some other recent acronyms (words formed from initial letters) have dropped the capital letters altogether:

*scuba:* Self-Contained Underwater Breathing Apparatus.

*laser:* Light Amplification by Stimulated Emission of Radiation. The laser beam has a great future.

*snafu:* Originally, Army slang for Situation Normal—All Fouled Up. The word, however, has gained respectability, being used frequently in newspaper headlines to describe a chaotic condition that was not altogether unexpected.

## The Comma

### A SUBSTITUTE FOR **AND** OR **OR**

One of the ways the comma serves as a shortcut is by replacing an *and* or an *or* in a series of words, phrases, or clauses. Notice the two ways in which the following sentences can be written:

| *Either* | *Or* |
|---|---|
| *a.* I bought eggs and cheese and bread and butter. | *a.* I bought eggs, cheese, bread, and butter. |
| *b.* He hopped and skipped and jumped his way down the street. | *b.* He hopped, skipped, and jumped his way down the street. |
| *c.* He walked on busy streets and signed postcards | *c.* He walked on busy streets, signed postcards bear- |

bearing his picture and shook hands all around.

*d.* This is as true of the doctor pondering a diagnosis or a lawyer studying a client's claims or a legislator weighing the merits of a new law.

*e.* This does not mean that all actions have been wise or that the emphasis has always been well judged or that things could not have been done differently.

ing his picture, and shook hands all around.

*d.* This is as true of a doctor pondering a diagnosis, a lawyer studying a client's claims, or a legislator weighing the merits of a new law.

*e.* This does not mean that all actions have been wise, that the emphasis has always been well judged, or that things could not have been done differently.

In *a* the nouns *eggs, cheese, bread,* and *butter* are called words in a series. In *b* we have the verbs *hopped, skipped,* and *jumped* as words in series. In *c* and *d* we have phrases in series and in *e* we have clauses in series. Usually there are at least three items of equal rank in a series. When we have such a series, whether it is made up of words, phrases, or dependent clauses, all items are separated from one another by commas. Even though we assume that the comma is used to take the place of *and* or *or,* its use is recommended even before the *and* between the last two items in the series so that these last two items may be considered separately, not in combination.

For example, when we say "The colors of our country are red, white, and blue," there's a little pause after *white* that seems to ask for a comma to make *blue* just as important as *red* and *white,* and not merely a combination of white and blue. This is a small point, admittedly. If you wish to follow the usage of *The New York Times,* most newspapers in the country, and the mass-circulation magazines,* you may omit the comma before *and* in a

* Mass-circulation magazines such as *Life, Time, Newsweek, Look, Reader's Digest* don't use the serial comma before *and* or *or. The New Yorker, Saturday Review, Atlantic Monthly, Harper's,* and *The New York Review of Books* do.

series. But be consistent. Either always leave out the comma before the last of the series or always put it in.

And by the way, always place a comma before *etc.* whether it is in a series or alone.

CAUTION

Don't, in your eagerness to insert a comma before the last item in a series, also put one after the last item.

Which comma is wrong in the following examples?

> The driver's inability, his lack of knowledge of his car, the condition of roads and traffic, and irresponsible recklessness, are the main causes of highway accidents.

> The President, his wife, the bride, the bridegroom, and all the principals, were present at the rehearsal today.

In both sentences, the last comma is wrong and should be eliminated.

### A REPLACEMENT FOR WORDS THAT ARE "UNDERSTOOD"

Sometimes the comma replaces other words that are easily understood:

> Chief, Division of Finance
> Chairman, English Department
> (In both cases, the words *of the* are left out.)

> Once we had much; now, nothing.
> (The comma stands for "we have.")

> Dave owns a Mustang; Harry, a Valiant.
> (The comma stands for "owns.")

## PUNCTUATION OF ADJECTIVES IN SERIES

1. By which statement would Mrs. Grant be more flattered?
   *a.* Mrs. Grant is a pretty generous woman.
   *b.* Mrs. Grant is a pretty, generous woman.

As can be seen above, two adjectives can constitute a series. We can say either:

> I exercise my rights as a free and independent American.
>
> or
>
> I exercise my rights as a free, independent American.

The comma is again a shortcut for *and*. That's really the guide to whether to use a comma between two consecutive adjectives. If you can connect the adjectives with *and* sensibly; if the adjectives are parallel, of equal significance —then the comma is used.

However, if you say, "He scaled a high brick wall easily," *high* and *brick* are not parallel. It is not a high *and* brick wall, but a brick wall that is high. Therefore no comma is used.

To sum it up, don't use a comma if the first adjective qualifies the meaning of the combination of the second adjective and noun, as in: large delivery truck, modern elementary school, a delicious chocolate ice-cream soda.

## EXERCISE IN USE OF COMMAS WITH ADJECTIVES

Below is a list of sentences and phrases to test your ingenuity. Place commas wherever you feel they are necessary. In some instances your placement of commas will be a matter of interpretation.

1. lapped by clean clear water
2. a strong advocate of the two-party political system

3. The induction of Casey Stengel and Ted Williams into Baseball's Hall of Fame will probably cause a monumental traffic jam in this quiet lakeside community.

4. a devastating aerial bombardment

5. to shut out the din of screaming high-pitched yells

6. indispensable to a full rich life

*Fine Point:*

When the adjectives follow the noun, the first adjective is separated from the noun by a comma: ***Without these he would have produced a textbook, dutiful, static, and virtually unreadable.***

## The Ellipsis

An ellipsis (. . .) is really a shortcut which says, "At this point we have omitted words that were in the original." If the incomplete quotation comes at the beginning of your sentence, three dots are used. If it comes at the end of one of your sentences, four dots are used—three dots for the incomplete quotation and one dot for the period that actually concludes your sentence.

The ellipsis is often used in advertising movies, books, or plays, when the advertiser wishes perhaps to leave out some less flattering intervening remarks:

> ". . . nears the edge of greatness."
> "This book has everything. . . ."

Advertisers for the big department stores like to lay down a barrage of ellipses between ecstatic phrases of fulsome praise of their products. Here's a not untypical sentence from a sales advertisement for fur-lined coats:

> Don't miss these rare values . . . now . . . when you need them most . . . not at the height of the cold wintry weather.

Nothing is left out—except the proper punctuation. The three dots often save the writer the trouble of deciding whether to use a comma, a dash, a colon, an exclamation point, or a period.

When gossip columnists and others have an assortment of rather short items they like to use ellipses to separate the items. The ellipsis is used instead of a new paragraph and thus saves space.

*The only need you will have for the ellipsis is in the writing of a research paper* in which you quote some authority and you use the three or four dots to show where you have omitted material that appeared in the original.

## THE COMMA AND THE DASH AS "SLOW" SIGNS

### The Comma

1. Which sentence shows extraordinary powers of persuasion?
   *a.* I left him convinced he was a fool.
   *b.* I left him, convinced he was a fool.

2. Which will require a lot of postage?
   *a.* Shall I stick the stamps on myself?
   *b.* Shall I stick the stamps on, myself?

3. Which headline is unfair to eight million people?
   *a.* POPULATION OF NEW YORK CITY, BROKEN DOWN BY AGE AND SEX
   *b.* POPULATION OF NEW YORK CITY BROKEN DOWN BY AGE AND SEX

4. Which is merely a repetition of information previously given?
   *a.* Again the temperature in New York City is 73.
   *b.* Again, the temperature in New York City is 73.

5. Which is a denial that politics had anything to do with the appointment?
   *a.* Joe did not get the appointment, because he was a Republican.
   *b.* Joe did not get the appointment because he was a Republican.

6. In which statement does the general command the larger number of marines?
   *a.* Lieut. Gen. Lewis W. Walt now commands 64,816 marines, more than took the field in the entire Korean war.
   *b.* Lieut. Gen. Lewis W. Walt now commands 64,816 marines more than took the field in the entire Korean war.

7. Which expresses disagreement tactfully?
   *a.* It isn't so, dear.
   *b.* It isn't so dear.

8. Which makes certainty seem an objective hard to attain?
   *a.* It's sometimes a little difficult to be sure.
   *b.* It's sometimes a little difficult, to be sure.

## THE COMMA AS A DIVIDER

We are dealing here only with the comma that divides, the comma that avoids collisions between words. The eight parallel sentences above show what a difference in meaning this comma can sometimes make.

### EXERCISE IN THE USE OF COMMAS FOR CLARITY

Through the use of a single comma make each of the following sentences immediately clear to the reader.

1. In writing such sentences need commas to make their meaning clear.

2. While I watched my father changed the back tire.

3. By the way things are going very well for me this year.

4. Just as I was about to leave my parents drove up in their car.

5. When he fired the bullet always hit the target.

6. As we understand the proposal does not undermine our commitments nor does it prejudge the results of the pending study.

7. If you can afford to go to St. Thomas for the Christmas vacation.

8. Despite its problems the region had managed to survive thanks to the Americans.

9. Hemingway captured the essence of what it is for a man to be alienated better than anyone writing today.

10. They recognize that the FBI's report was by no means complete and say it could not have been given the time and circumstances.

The first seven sentences in the exercise follow the pattern of having words, phrases, or dependent clauses come before the main thought. Therefore, we need to

use a comma to avoid a collision between two words that should not be run (or read) together.

When commas were more frequently used, there was a

rule that all dependent clauses (like the *when* clause in this sentence) had to be set off from the main clause by a comma. Today the writer uses his judgment, inserting the comma only when he thinks it will be of some help to the reader. However, if you are in doubt, you may use a comma whenever the dependent clause comes first. It isn't wrong. It's just not always needed. It's an "optional comma."

When the dependent clause* comes after the main clause, we do not ordinarily use the comma to separate the main from the dependent clause:

> I'll tell you when I see you. (No comma)
>
> When I see you, I'll tell you. (The comma is optional, though unnecessary and a bit wasteful.)

A mere reading of these two sentences will show you why. You can slow down if you wish to in your reading of the second sentence after the word *you,* but no such slowing down is indicated in the first sentence.

Exceptions? Of course! *Though* and *although* seem to be special and whether they come fore or aft I have seen commas used almost always.

### SOME FINE POINTS

> He did not get the appointment because he was a Republican.

This sentence, without a comma before *because,* means that he got the appointment on merit, not because he was a Republican. Put the comma before *because* and the

---

* A dependent clause—in case you've forgotten—is a sentence whose independence has been destroyed by placing a conjunction like *if, when, because, although,* etc. in front of it. *I see you* is a sentence but *if I see you, when I see you,* etc. are no longer sentences; they are dependent clauses. They now need a main clause to complete them: *If I see you I'll tell you.* There are also *who, which,* and *that* clauses.

sentence charges that he was discriminated against because he belonged to the wrong party—because he was a Republican.

Conjunctions like *as, since,* and *while* when they follow the main clause do not have a comma before them when only time is meant. But if some other meaning is expressed, a comma is often helpful to the reader. It warns him that *time* is not meant. Look at the following sentences:

> He arrived *as* I left. (Time)
>
> I applauded, *as* did everyone else in the audience. (Other meaning than time)
>
> I haven't seen him *since* he was five years old. (Time)
>
> I won't tell him anything, *since* he is a person you can't trust with a secret. (Here *since* means *because.*)
>
> I'm going to sit here and watch you *while* you write that letter. (Time)
>
> We went to the movies, *while* the rest of the gang preferred to watch the Mets' game. (*While* equals *whereas.*)

Too much for you? Forget it! Instead, remember the old rhyme:

> When in doubt
> Leave it out.

### THE COMMA WITH PARTICIPIAL PHRASES

When the participial phrase comes first, as it often does, we not only put a comma after the phrase but we must be careful to make sure that the word after the comma is the doer or the receiver of the action expressed in the participle.

There are three things to remember here:

1. Place a comma after an introductory participial phrase.

2. Make sure the next word is the doer or receiver of the action of the participle.

3. If the participial phrase comes at the end of the sentence a comma precedes it *if the participle refers to the subject of the sentence.*

"I left him, convinced he was a fool" means that *I* was convinced he was a fool. The comma shows that *convinced* and *him* are not to be read together. The omission of the comma in "I left him convinced he was a fool" means that I was able to convince *him* that he was a fool.

## THE COMMA AT OTHER SLOW-DOWN POINTS

Whenever the relationship of words anywhere in the sentence can be or needs to be made clearer by a slow-down signal, use a comma.

1. If the sentence adds a concluding question (like the French *n'est-ce pas?*) we use a comma:

> You wouldn't do that, would you?
>
> You're sure, aren't you?
>
> It's true, isn't it?

2. When a phrase introduced by *not* comes at the end of a sentence, a comma should precede it to show the break:

> The talk in Hollywood studios is about TV, *not* movies.
>
> A great number of movies are being made this summer but the action is in Europe, *not* in Hollywood.

3. To avoid confusion use a comma between side-by-side repetition of the same word or phrase in a sentence:

> Too many people who suffer, suffer alone.

4. When a word is repeated for emphasis, a comma is desirable:

> It took place many, many years ago.
>
> I found the incident very, very funny.

5. Use a comma to separate a quoted sentence from the phrase *he said* or its equivalent:

> Charles pleaded, "Give me another chance."
>
> "Please try to be there," Susan begged.

6. Although various punctuation marks may be used *before* expressions like *namely, for example,* and *that is,* be careful to use a comma after them.

> We don't want to ignore the clear need of the United Nations for adequate authority if it is to do its original job: *namely,* to maintain the peace of the world.
>
> It is a work of infinite complexity; you will find, *for example,* a total of eight intricate variations on the same theme.
>
> I really can't make it—*that is,* I'd like to come, but it's impossible this weekend.

7. When the month, day, and year are given, the accepted practice is to put commas after the day and the year:

> On October 14, 1966, the town of Hastings celebrated the anniversary of the famous battle fought there in 1066.
>
> The Atomic Age began July 16, 1945, about fifty air miles from Alamogordo, New Mexico.

When only the month and year are given, the favored practice is to leave the commas out:

> I started school in September 1958.

8. In writing addresses commas are used between each of the various items in the address and a final comma is used after the last item in the address. Commas are always used around the state or the country when it follows the name of the city.

> Please write to me at 1750 Newcastle Road, Tulsa, Oklahoma, after you have reached a decision.
>
> Cliff and Nancy Richey of San Angelo, Texas, made history today by becoming the first brother and sister to win national singles championships in the same year.

9. To avoid confusion, commas are placed between numbers in situations like the following:

> Instead of 12, 24 appeared at the party.
>
> In 1930, 400 men were dismissed.

10. For convenience in reading we separate hundreds, thousands, millions, billions, etc., with commas:

> 4,572 42,691 91,567,000

## THE COMMA IN THE COMPOUND SENTENCE

Where, in the following sentences, would you place a comma so that the meaning is clear to the reader?

1. The gallery has been carpeted with artificial grass and some large potted plants have been introduced to help the visitor visualize the sculpture in a natural site.

2. In the afternoon Penn State will meet San Francisco and Villanova will take on St. John's.

3. Mrs. Harriet Craig was interested only in her home and keeping her husband's love didn't seem to be as important to her.

4. All the houses are one-family homes with neat little gardens around them and trees line the street on both sides.

5. We saw them both yesterday afternoon and last night we had a theater date together.

6. Nolan Ryan walked Brooks Robinson and Frank Robinson hit a home run over the right-field wall.

7. I went to the theater with my mother and my sister went to the ballet with my father.

8. One division is guarding the supply lines between the two forces and patrols are scattered throughout the area.

In the sentences you have just punctuated, two statements of equal importance are connected by *and*. We call such sentences compound sentences because they have two independent clauses.

There used to be a hard-and-fast rule about sentences connected by the coordinating conjunctions *and, but, or,* and *nor:* If you had a sentence on each side of the conjunction, a comma was used.

S S
———, and ———

S S
———, but ———

The comma before *and* and *or,* however, is gradually disappearing. Very often one sees the comma only when both parts are rather long or when a misinterpretation might result if a comma were not used. There are many compound *and* and *or* sentences where no comma is used.

> Ernest Hemingway had loved firearms all his adult life and it may have been fitting that he received his

death from one yesterday morning at Sun Valley, Idaho.

If you are uncertain about leaving out the comma, you may use commas before the *and* or *or* in all compound sentences. With *but* and *nor* the comma appears more frequently because of the negative nature of the conjunctions.

With *for*, the use of the comma is strongly recommended in order to give the sentence immediate clarity. It is easy to see that with a sentence like "I shall remember him for his kindness gave me my first start," a comma before *for* would help to make the meaning of the sentence clearer.

**CAUTION**

Do not use the comma before *and* or *or* unless there is a complete sentence on each side of the conjunction. Don't use a comma between two nouns, two verbs, two phrases, or two dependent clauses connected by *and, or,* or even *but*. WORRY ABOUT THIS; DON'T WORRY ABOUT PUTTING THE COMMA BEFORE *AND* IN COMPOUND SENTENCES.

### EXERCISE IN USE OF COMMA BEFORE CONJUNCTIONS

In the following sentences indicate whether the comma before *and, but, or,* and *for* is:

1. wrong
2. optional (not really necessary but all right to use)
3. necessary for immediate clarity

Examples of the three different kinds:

I don't like his superior attitude, and his witless remarks. (Wrong. Here *and* separates two nouns, not two sentences.)

I don't like his superior attitude, and I don't care for his witless remarks. (Optional. Though the comma is not necessary—even though separating two sentences—some people feel safer using it.)

I don't like his superior attitude, and his witless remarks make me writhe. (Necessary if you want to make the sentence immediately clear to the reader.)

1. He urged the President to withdraw his personal approval, or at least hold up export licenses for the tractors.

2. Major Collins became the first man to go outside his spacecraft more than once, and on the second excursion he became the first man to retrieve an object from another satellite.

3. A dispute between Oxford dons is always something the British enjoy, and there is added relish when the clash is between two of Britain's most prominent historians.

4. The trouble is that the government is promising more than it has to give, and is acting without a set of priorities.

5. Matthew Arnold believed that literature is a criticism of life, and that literature is valueless unless it illuminates our understanding of ourselves and the universe that surrounds us.

6. By 1974 the supersonic jetliner will be as long as a football field, and capable of carrying 500 persons from one place to another at 1,800 miles per hour.

7. He protested that he had been a soldier under orders, and that the legal guilt lay with those who had given the orders.

8. He performed his task with efficiency, and evident enthusiasm.

9. Altogether there are seventeen white tigers alive in captivity, and only three have found their way outside India.

10. The present exhibition affords immense pleasure, for it illustrates why Gainsborough was considered one of the most impressive artists of his period.

## Trends in Comma Usage

A sentence that needs too many commas is a poor sentence—no matter who writes it. And having said that, I'm going to stick my neck out a little further and quote a sentence* taken almost at random from *The Turn of the Screw* by Henry James:

> This person proved, on her presenting herself, for judgment, at a house in Harley Street, that impressed her as vast and imposing—this prospective patron proved a gentleman, a bachelor in the prime of life, such a figure as had never risen, save in a dream or an old novel, before a fluttered, anxious girl out of a Hampshire vicarage.†

No modern writer would use any of the first four commas James used—or need to. For example, here's a sentence from *The New York Times* of September 10, 1966:

> The parents of one of five boys barred from regular classes at the high school here because their hair is long said today that their son had not told the truth when he said that they supported his refusal to cut his hair.

Nary a comma and clear as crystal!

So even if you read no further in this section I can say something very important to you:

Use commas sparingly. Don't make them crutches on

* From *The Two Magics* by Henry James, reprinted by permission of The Macmillan Co.

† So far as punctuation is concerned, this sentence is not unfair to Henry James. A study made by Professor George Summey, Jr. (*Modern Punctuation*, Oxford University Press), shows that Henry James uses 6.8 marks of punctuation per sentence, second in this respect to Walter Pater.

which your sentence has to lean. A good sentence should be able to stand on its own feet. One of the chief purposes of this section is to get you to use fewer commas and to use those few more effectively.

Gore Vidal put it very well when he recently wrote: "As to commas, those of us brought up on Fowler used to allow them to swarm like gnats upon the page. Now the comma is used sparingly and I prefer the new economy."

## THE DASH

> One of the most eye-catching signals is the dash, used chiefly and dramatically to imitate the spontaneity of speech—the sudden hesitation, the switching of controls that give the emphasis of gestures. Emily Dickinson (who hoarded so much drama) was full of dashes. And so was Conrad. "Mistah Kurtz—he dead."
>
> —NONA BALAKIAN in *The New York Times* November 27, 1965

Which is a warning intended for drivers?

a. Go slow—children.
b. Go slow, children.

As can be seen, the dash—a more dramatic slow-down mark of punctuation than a comma—generally signals a sharper turn. It is a versatile mark of punctuation that can be used to make an abrupt turn in thought, to emphasize a remark, to introduce a summary, or to add suspense. It sometimes even says, "Look out; something surprising or amusing is coming."

Here are some examples of sentences using a dash. Notice the use of the dash in each of these sentences:

1. "We were up over four hundred miles," Commander Young of Gemini 10 said, "and Columbus was right—the world is round."

2. Among the first things a traveler notes on entering Rumania is that the airport signs carry information in English, Rumanian, French, and Italian—not Russian.

3. Freedom of speech, freedom of worship, freedom from want, freedom from fear—these are the fundamentals of a moral world order.

4. Yesterday President De Gaulle spoke to a cheering crowd in Cambodia, but much of what he said was intended for a different audience—Americans.

5. We need more money for housing, health, hospitals—every area of public life.

6. City Patrolman Boyce McCall says a man he sought to arrest for drunkenness followed the lead of his dog—and bit him.

7. "Then I went up to this other fellow who was looking at me—but you're not listening!"

8. The year 1985 may well see man's greatest crisis, a crisis in performing an elementary task—feeding himself.

9. He who laughs—lasts.

10. To be or not to be, that is—the infinitive.

## CAUTION

It's very tempting to use the dash. Don't overuse it. Don't use it where a comma would be just as effective. Always have some legitimate or important reason for doing so. Use dashes sparingly—and therefore effectively.

# DETOUR

## DETOURS USING COMMAS, DASHES, PARENTHESES, AND BRACKETS

### Commas

In the following sentences notice how commas affect meaning.

1. Which indicates that there were only two people in the car?
   *a.* The two passengers who were seriously hurt were taken to a nearby hospital.
   *b.* The two passengers, who were seriously hurt, were taken to a nearby hospital.

2. In which has the speaker pried into the private lives of his friends?
   *a.* Everyone I know has a secret ambition.
   *b.* Everyone, I know, has a secret ambition.

3. Which sentence has cannibalistic overtones?
   *a.* We are going to eat, John, before we take another step.
   *b.* We are going to eat John before we take another step.

4. Which is a matter of identification?
   *a.* He is the one, I believe.
   *b.* He is the one I believe.

5. Which is the dedication of a self-confessed polygamist?
   *a.* I dedicate this book to my wife, Edith, for telling me what to leave out.
   *b.* I dedicate this book to my wife Edith for telling me what to leave out.

6. If a Democrat were President, which prediction would forecast a change in administration?
   *a.* The Republicans, say the Democrats, are sure to win the next Presidential election.
   *b.* The Republicans say the Democrats are sure to win the next Presidential election.

7. In which case is the Prime Minister probably feeling more alone?
   *a.* The Prime Minister, who was recently ousted by the Korean citizens and his wife, arrived in Hawaii yesterday.
   *b.* The Prime Minister, who was recently ousted by the Korean citizens, and his wife arrived in Hawaii yesterday.

8. In which case has the speaker managed to change his friends' attitude toward him?
   *a.* Now, my friends, listen to me.
   *b.* Now my friends listen to me.

9. Which is the neurotic personality?
   *a.* She too eagerly awaits the spring.
   *b.* She, too, eagerly awaits the spring.

10. Which is a blanket endorsement of all Democratic candidates?
   *a.* The President urged voters to elect Democratic senators and congressmen, who would be sure to support his program to the hilt.
   *b.* The President urged voters to elect Democratic senators and congressmen who would be sure to support his program to the hilt.

## COMMAS WITH NONESSENTIAL CLAUSES AND PHRASES

Sometimes commas, instead of being used *between* words (like the single commas discussed in the preceding chapter), are used *around* words, phrases, or clauses to indicate a detour from the main thought. Two commas are needed for such detours (when they occur within the sentence): one comma to show at what point we begin the detour, the other to show at what point we return to the main road of the sentence. Such commas are like (parentheses) or [brackets]. You always need a pair of them. They fence in or enclose in much the same way as parentheses and brackets do, but to a lesser degree.

Let us look more closely at several sentences and see what actually happens when detours from the main road occur. The following sentence consists only of a main road: there are no detours.

> The subcontinent of India can someday become one of the world's great powers.

This sentence is the main road for sentences a, b, c, d, and e that follow.

> a. The subcontinent of India, *a nation of more than 500 million people,* can someday become one of the world's great powers.

The phrase *a nation of more than 500 million people* is a detour. It is not an essential part of the main thought; it does not identify India. It can be left out without changing the meaning of the sentence. We, therefore, fence it in with commas to leave the main road clear. Technically, we call *a nation . . . people* a phrase in apposition or an appositive phrase.

If we were to diagram this sentence it would look something like this:

The subcontinent of India — — — — — — — — — —

can someday become one of the world's great

powers.

The heavy black line indicates the main road, or main thought. The broken line indicates the detour, *a nation of more than 500 million people*. The arrows show where the commas are used—one to take us off the main road, the other to bring us back on to it, thus keeping the lines of communication open between the two parts of the main road of the sentence.

> b. The subcontinent of India, *inhabited by more than 500 million people,* can someday become one of the world's great powers.

Here in b the detour words, *inhabited by more than 500 million people,* are again not an essential part of the sentence. Therefore, we put commas around them. Technically, *inhabited . . . people* is called a participial phrase.

> c. The subcontinent of India, *which has a population of 500 million people,* can someday become one of the world's great powers.

The detour in c is a relative clause introduced by the relative pronoun *which.*

> d. The subcontinent of India, *ladies and gentlemen,* can someday become one of the world's great powers.

This sentence is evidently part of a speech. The interrupting words, the detour *ladies and gentlemen,* are said to be in direct address. All words in direct address are detours; they don't affect the main thought of the sentence. Notice, however, that if *ladies and gentlemen* came first only one comma would be needed—after *gentlemen.* If *ladies and gentlemen* came at the end of the sentence there would be only one comma—before *ladies.* The complementary commas have, in one case, been absorbed by the capital letter at the beginning of the sentence; in the other case, by the period at the end of the sentence.

> e. The subcontinent of India, *in my opinion,* can someday become one of the world's great powers.

*In my opinion* is a parenthetical expression, an interrupter, thrust into the sentence. We, therefore, place detour commas around it. Other parenthetical phrases or clauses that might have been used and would generally be fenced in by commas are *I think, I believe, I'm sure, I know, if I may be permitted to venture an opinion,* etc. All such interrupters of the main flow of thought, all such detours from the main road, are marked off with commas.

### NO COMMAS WITH ESSENTIAL CLAUSES

Not all *who* or *which* clauses are detours. Sometimes they are essential parts of the main thought; they identify what has gone before, as in the following sentence:

> Milk which has been allowed to stand in the sun for a long time is unfit to drink.

If we place detour commas around the relative clause *which has been allowed to stand in the sun for a long time,* the main thought becomes *Milk is unfit to drink,* which is obviously nonsense and is not what the sentence intends to say. The sentence means that only a certain kind of milk is unfit to drink. Therefore the relative clause *which . . . time* is essential to the thought of the sentence;

it identifies the kind of milk—not any milk but only that which has been exposed to the sun for a long time.

It is interesting to note that we can substitute *that* for *which;* indeed, *that* was at one time the relative pronoun used in sentences like this one. The pronoun *that* helps to point or identify.

For example, in the sentence, "George Washington, who was our first President, is still one of our national heroes," it would be impossible to substitute *that* for *who.* George Washington is already sufficiently identified. On the other hand, in the sentence, "The George Washington who lives on our block says he is a direct descendant of our first President," we could substitute *that* for *who* and we would use no commas. The *who* (or *that*) *lives on our block* is essential, for it identifies the particular George Washington we're talking about.

## EXERCISE IN USE OF COMMAS WITH RELATIVE CLAUSES

The following sentences have all been taken from newspapers and magazines, but the commas around nonessential relative clauses have been removed. Examine these sentences and put commas around the nonessential relative clauses. Be sure you use two commas unless the nonessential clause comes at the end of a sentence; then you would only use one comma before the first word in the clause. Whenever you are in doubt—when you are not sure whether a clause is essential or not—leave out the commas.

*Hint:* If you can substitute *that* for *who* or *which,* you can be pretty sure that the clause is essential or identifying and that no commas are needed. Further hint: Sometimes *when* means "at which time" and *where* means "at which place" and are, therefore, treated in the same way as relative pronouns.

1. Humphrey Bogart who was a popular movie star in his own time and has become a legend since his death is the subject of a new biography called *Bogie.*

2. Students who chose voluntarily to go to summer school did so to lighten their credit loads in the next semester.

3. Severe economic measures have been threatened against Cuban workers who fail to learn to read or write by the end of this year.

4. Many of the fountains which were ordered shut down are again flowing.

5. Leontyne Price who may possess the most beautiful soprano voice on the musical stage today could scarcely have sung more gloriously than she did last night.

6. The Navy pilot who escaped from a North Vietnamese prison and reached safety after a twenty-three-day trek through the jungle was identified today as Lt. Dieter Dengler.

7. Lt. Dengler's brother Martin who works in a bakery in San Francisco was very happy when he got the news.

8. Extra policemen have been concentrated at two trouble spots since Thursday night when an eleven-year-old boy was slain in the street after a clash between two rival youth groups.

9. Hiroshima which was destroyed by the world's first atom bomb observed the event today with names still being added to the list of victims.

10. Last month's disastrous floods which severely damaged so many Italian works of art contributed to the discovery of an ancient fresco in Pisa.

## COMMAS WITH PARTICIPIAL AND APPOSITIVE PHRASES

Participial and appositive phrases must be tested, as subordinate clauses are, to determine whether they are essential and identifying or are merely giving additional information. Notice the participial phrase in the following sentence:

> The man crossing the street is my uncle.

We use no commas to enclose this participial phrase because *crossing the street* identifies the man. It is saying "Not any man, but the one *crossing the street* is my uncle."

Now examine the function of the participial phrase in the following sentence:

> My uncle Jack, *crossing the street carelessly,* met with an accident.

We use commas here because *my uncle Jack* is sufficiently identified, and the participial phrase *crossing the street carelessly* merely gives additional information about him. It does not identify.

In which of the two following sentences would you not use commas to enclose the appositive phrase?

1. John Keats the great English poet died when he was only twenty-six.
2. The great English poet John Keats died when he was only twenty-six.

Obviously, no commas are used in the second sentence because *John Keats* identifies which one of the great English poets, of whom there are many, is meant. In the first sentence, however, the detour commas are used. The phrase *the great English poet* supplies additional information for the uninformed.

> Who has more than one brother: A or B?
> A: My brother David is going with me.
> B: My brother, David, is going with me.

A says that only his brother David is going with him; his other brother or brothers are staying at home.

B says—when we remove what's between the detour commas—that his brother is going with him. B has no other brothers. His brother's name happens to be David.

*Note:* A related but slightly different use of the detour comma is seen in the following sentences. Notice that commas enclose the phrases introduced by *or*. These "*or* phrases" give a brief definition of what has gone before.

> This year the excavations will continue in the agora, *or marketplace,* of ancient Corinth.
>
> New Testament Greek was not that of Aristotle or Euripides, but rather the "Koine" Greek that was the lingua franca, or unifying language, of the Roman Empire.

## EXERCISE I. DOUBLE OR NOTHING: COMMAS WITH APPOSITIVE PHRASES

The following sentences, taken from newspapers and magazines, all contain appositive phrases. The commas, however, have been removed. Read these sentences and insert commas wherever you feel they are necessary. (Not all of the sentences require commas.) Remember that to make a detour with words or phrases in apposition you need two commas (except at the end of a sentence) thus keeping the lines of communication open. Be sure, too, that you put the second comma in the right place, for what is left after you remove the words surrounded by commas should make complete sense.

1. Al Kelly one of the few public speakers to use double talk on purpose will receive an award on Sunday.

2. Spaghetti and meatballs once a strictly Italian dish now has become the seventh most popular fare in the United States.

3. A coelacanth one of the oldest species of fish in the world and very rarely caught was recently shipped to the United States in a refrigerated box.

4. The American freighter *Export Buyer* brought the specimen to the United States.

5. The meaning of neutrality a rather straightforward business for the man in the street but an involved affair for diplomats is what the conference is all about.

6. Astrology the art of predicting events from the location of the stars and planets is one of the oldest professions in India.

7. *Elizabeth and Essex* a play by the poet and playwright Maxwell Anderson was revived at the City Center last night.

8. Digging to discover the site of Camelot court of King Arthur and his knights of the Round Table will start soon near a Somerset village.

9. The poet and playwright Bertolt Brecht may be considered to have made the major German contribution to world literature in our time.

10. Joseph Priestley of England and Antoine Lavoisier of France eighteenth-century contemporaries are generally considered to be the fathers of modern science.

## EXERCISE II. PLACEMENT OF COMMAS FOR CLARITY

I found the following mispunctuated sentences in print. The only liberty I have taken is to shorten some of them. What you have to do is (1) insert a missing comma, (2) take a comma already there and put it where it belongs, or (3) remove a comma that is not altogether necessary. Notice that the use of one comma where two (a pair) are needed acts as a roadblock. The lines of communication are cut and are not restored until we put in the other comma.

*Check:* After you enclose a clause or phrase in commas, can you read what's left outside the commas and does it make sense? If it does not, the commas probably should not be used.

1. Driving a car in London he found out, was a nightmarish experience.

2. The author, one of the most thoughtful and literate of jazz critics has just completed a new book on the subject.

3. Diplomatic observers though taken by surprise by General Mobutu's charges, indicated they had noticed an unusual degree of political agitation in the city during recent days.

4. All living creatures, no matter how small or insignificant were treated with kindness and respect by Dr. Albert Schweitzer.

5. According to Dr. Spotnitz, group psychotherapy constitutes the third Psychiatric Revolution—the previous two being symbolized by Philippe Pinel (1745–1826), the French specialist in mental disease and Sigmund Freud.

6. These diplomats feel that the American delegation, to NATO headed by Ambassador Harlan Cleveland, spent all its energy ineffectively.

7. The aspiring teacher must be fairly, if not thoroughly versed, in gathering information for a talk.

8. This makes it difficult for the two leaders, when they move from the realm of television generalities to the hard realities of political facts and military defense to agree on what to do.

9. For many years the prevailing opinion among educators was that while parents could help prepare children for later learning, the actual teaching should be left to teachers.

10. The Surgeon General regrets that despite two and a half years of intensive educational efforts, half of the nation's teen-agers are smoking by the time they are eighteen.

## Dashes, Parentheses, and Brackets

Dashes — —, parentheses ( ), and brackets [ ] are used for material that is obviously or strongly a detour from or an interruption of the main thought of the sentence.

### DASHES

In the following sentence there is a major detour, a break in the thought. The writer, therefore, uses dashes rather than commas to contain it.

> The auditor—shall we call him a knave or a fool?—approved an inaccurate statement.

Often where the significance of detour commas might not be clear we use dashes to make reading easier. In the following sentence dashes are used around the appositional phrase because the phrase itself already contains several commas.

> As a statement of the principal environmental issues confronting the nation—water pollution, air pollution, inadvertent modifications of weather and climate, disposal of solid wastes, problems of land use and of noise, pesticides and radiation—this article is lucid, comprehensive, useful.

### PARENTHESES

> The old-fashioned method of putting in a comma (or even a stronger stop) whenever a reader would naturally pause to take a breath when reading aloud (as at this point in this sentence) has little reason to recommend it.
>
> —*Chambers Encyclopedia* (1891)

Though detour commas might have been used for the first parentheses in the quotation above, the second interjection requires parentheses. Note also the parentheses around 1891. Enclosure of dates is one of the chief uses of this mark of punctuation.

## BRACKETS

Brackets around words in a quotation indicate that the words so bracketed do not appear in the original quotation or citation. They have been put in by the person quoting or citing them in order to give information to the reader.

> "He [John Adams] was weak in punctuation," said his great-great-great-grandson [Thomas Boylston Adams], "but strong in everything else."
>
> —Quoted from *The New Yorker*

*Sic* is a Latin word meaning "thus" or "so." In English it most often comes wrapped in brackets. When tossed into a quoted passage the [*sic*] points an accusing finger at the word immediately before it and says to the reader: "This is the way it appeared in the original. Don't hold me responsible for this misspelling or misuse. I know better."

On rare occasions when it is necessary to have parentheses within parentheses, brackets are used for the inner parentheses.

### EXERCISE IN CHOICE OF DETOUR MARKS

In the following sentences, indicate whether to use detour commas, dashes, parentheses, brackets, or nothing around the italicized words. Watch the *if* clauses especially —sometimes they are essential and it is better not to have detour commas around them. Justify your choice, remembering that sometimes one choice may be as good as another. Just be sure you have a good reason.

1. The groups in which we grow up and live *family, school, community, profession, etc.* exert a profound influence on us.

2. Other archaeologists are extremely cautious and believe that *although they appear to be very old* the tools found may be much more recent.

3. Behind every great achievement *the building of the Pyramids, the winning of a war for liberty, the creation of new machines, the revelation of inventions* stands a great mass of anonymous persons.

4. "It seems possible," Professor Robinson said, "that this head is from an acrolithic statue *a statue with head and extremities of stone* and that the wooden body as well as the back of the marble head was covered by real drapery." (The italicized words were not part of Professor Robinson's statement.)

5. The Italian border province of Alto Adige *called South Tyrol by Austrians* has a German-speaking majority.

6. Wellington was a truly remarkable man; success *and he was prodigious in terms of both achievement and worldly reward* never altered him a jot.

7. The government is trying hard *too hard, according to some critics* to attract more foreign tourists.

8. Five leaders in arts and journalism *Aaron Copland, Arthur M. Schlesinger, Jr., Archibald MacLeish, James Reston, and Robert Penn Warren* discussed the future of their fields.

9. The bronze is a life-size head of a boy *some scholars say it is a youthful portrait of the Emperor Nero* and is dated from the first century.

10. An eminent British archaeologist said today he was "almost certain" that Camelot *King Arthur's legendary castle* had been found.

11. If baseball men are smart *and this is sometimes doubted greatly* they'll never let him go.

12. A knuckleball *the most difficult pitch to throw* has no spin.

## THE SEMICOLON AND THE COLON AS "SLOW" SIGNS

### The Semicolon

> And what of the semicolon? Is it really to be scrapped? Not, surely, while there are writers around whose ideas follow a lateral pattern, who no sooner finish a thought than they feel another of equal weight emerging—all leading to a final note of elucidation.
>
> —NONA BALAKIAN in *The New York Times* November 27, 1965

Peter Quennell is a contemporary British biographer (of Shakespeare and Byron) and an essayist who writes some of today's best prose. In his book of essays called *The Sign of the Fish*, Quennell uses 4.5 semicolons per page. (I counted forty-five semicolons on pages 120 to 129 inclusive.) Walter Kerr, drama critic of *The New York Times,* in his article of October 23, 1966, called "While a Novel Can Roam, a Play Must Stay Home," used fourteen semicolons.

Quennell and Kerr must be among those writers "who no sooner finish a thought than they feel another of equal weight emerging."

#### THE SEMICOLON'S MAIN FUNCTION

A semicolon is like the fulcrum on an old-fashioned pair of scales, balancing the equal weights on each side of it.

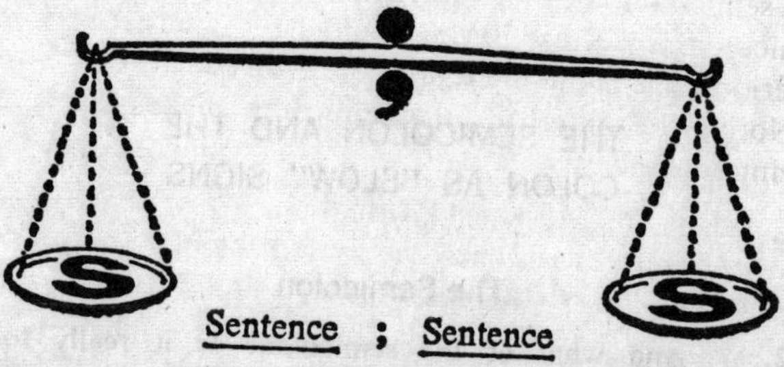

Here is a recent example of just such a sentence from a speech made by Hubert H. Humphrey to a gathering of college students:

> Knowledge without commitment is wasteful;
> Commitment without knowledge is dangerous.

The two ideas are equally balanced with the semicolon acting as the fulcrum. The thought could also have been written.

> Knowledge without commitment is wasteful, and commitment without knowledge is dangerous.

or

> Knowledge without commitment is wasteful. Commitment without knowledge is dangerous.

Of these three ways of expressing the thought which do you think is the most effective? My vote goes to the one with the semicolon; there's a kind of inevitability to it—a swiftness, a strength, a vigorous balance of ideas that the other two somehow lack.

A semicolon, then, is used to separate (and, paradoxically, at the same time connect) two or more closely connected thoughts where you feel that a comma plus *and* would weaken their effectiveness or a period would keep them too far apart. This is the chief function and use of the semicolon. It is a safe rule to say that you know a semicolon is correct if you could have alternatively used a period to separate the sentences involved.

Notice the difference the semicolon makes in the following sentences:

1. Which officials should be dismissed?
   *a.* Seven officials knew the secret, all told.
   *b.* Seven officials knew the secret; all told.
2. Which headline has a taint of cannibalism about it?
   *a.* Senate group eats chickens, cabinet wives, sweetbreads.
   *b.* Senate group eats chickens; cabinet wives, sweetbreads.

Here again you can see that in each of the sentences a period could have been used instead of a semicolon.

> Seven officials knew the secret. All told.
> Senate group eats chicken. Cabinet wives (eat) sweetbreads.

OTHER USES OF THE SEMICOLON

1. There are certain connecting words and phrases such as *however, therefore, nevertheless, consequently, moreover, besides, indeed, in fact, of course, on the contrary,* etc. that need more than a comma to separate them from the preceding sentence.

It is not considered good punctuation to write:

> Their aims and ideals seem admirable, however, their methods are questionable.

You can see that this sentence, thus punctuated, lacks instant clarity: you read past the word *however* before you realize that another thought is beginning. It is in such cases that the semicolon is useful. We can write this sentence in one of two ways:

> Their aims and ideals seem admirable; however, their methods are questionable.

or

> Their aims and ideals seem admirable. However, their methods are questionable.

There is a growing tendency to place the *however* within the second sentence, thus:

> Their aims and ideals seem admirable. Their methods, however, are questionable.

2. Where sentences are short and all deal with a continuing idea, we may have semicolons in series. The general practice is to use the semicolon before the final *and*, as this sentence shows:

> By October, publishers are committed; the catalogues have been distributed; the advertising campaign is under way; the bookstores are ordering; and even such peripheral members of the trade as reviewers and critics have a fairly good idea of what is coming.

3. When the items in series are clauses that already have commas, the semicolon is sometimes used as a stronger barrier between the clauses in series:

> The teachers-to-be, working with experts and simultaneously with schoolchildren, are learning how soil absorbs moisture or, if it is hard-packed, shunts it aside; how trees and plants survive; and how some of the most fascinating studies of nature can be carried on in a houselot, a city park, or even a schoolyard.

4. When either or both of the thoughts in a compound sentence *(and, but, or, nor, for)* already have commas the need for a stronger and less confusing mark than a comma is sometimes indicated:

> His nation ought to get—in our interest as well as theirs—all the help we can give them; and they ought to get it, as the President proposes to give it, without strings or political interference.

It is easy to see that a comma before *and* would be overwhelmed by both halves of the sentence; therefore, a stronger barrier—the semicolon—is used to avoid confusion.

5. When a series ordinarily using commas has commas within the items, then again a less confusing barrier, the semicolon, is advisable:

> Besides Mr. Rogers and Mr. Sisco, the relief conference included Samuel DePalma, Assistant Secretary of State for International Organization Affairs; George Bush, the chief United States delegate; and Francis L. Kellogg, a special assistant to Mr. Rogers for refugee and migration affairs.

## The Colon

> I was startled to find out how much I—and others—used the colon in the Forties. Like a blare of French horns introducing a significant theme, the colon was used almost as much (and as irritatingly) as Sterne's dashes.
>
> —Gore Vidal

The colon is used a great deal today and in just the way that Gore Vidal has so eloquently described: "like a blare of French horns introducing a significant theme." That's how the colon differs from the semicolon: it introduces, it supplements, it explains, it adds something that is a part of what the sentence itself is saying or it is related to it. On the other hand, the semicolon in its chief use separates; it separates two sentences closely connected in thought and is virtually equivalent to a period between those sentences.

Diagramed, the difference between the semicolon and colon looks like this:

SEMICOLON

Sentence ; Sentence.
Sentence ; however, Sentence.
Sentence (with comma) ; and Sentence.

COLON

Sentence* : one word completing thought.

1. The reaction of the New York Mets to the billiard-table surface now used for an outfield in the Astrodome can be summed up in one word: *phooey.*

Sentence* : a phrase.

2. All the main economic indicators point the same way: toward a tapering off of the upward climb of the economy.

Sentence* : dependent clause.

3. Everybody agrees on one thing: that the present trend of policy has to be changed.

Sentence* : Sentence.

4. Yet there was no clear answer to the question: How could either side back away without losing face?

Notice that when a sentence follows the colon: 1) It is still a part of the initial thought and 2) It may begin with a capital letter especially when it is a question. (An initial capital letter is *never* used after a semicolon.)

* Note: The sentence to the left of the colon need not be totally completed or specific in meaning; indeed, it's what follows the colon that often completes the thought.

Another way of looking at the use of the colon is to realize that the colon is always used when the word *following* appears in the initial sentence:

> Please send me the following articles: three ball-point pens, two boxes of paper clips, and a box of carbon paper.

If the word *following* does not appear, it is generally implied. Look back at the four sentences given above and you will see that in each of them the word *following* could be substituted or supplied for what is there.

> Sentence 1: "summed up in the (following) word"
> Sentence 2: "point the (following) way"
> Sentence 3: "agrees on (the following) thing"
> Sentence 4: "answer to the (following) question"

**CAUTION**

Don't use a colon after the word *are* if the items are immediately listed.

> His good qualities are honesty, integrity, and courage. (In this sentence *honesty, integrity,* and *courage* are predicate nouns.)

Only if tabulation occurs or if the word *following* appears, do we use the colon after a form of the verb *to be.* (In tabulation, capitals are often used for each item.)

> The three pillars we must build on are:
> A strong economy;
> A sense of duty; and
> A spacious vision.

## OTHER USES OF THE COLON

Other uses of the colon are purely arbitrary. They are:

1. To indicate time, separating the minutes from the hour.

> It is now 12:30 P.M.

2. After *he said,* etc., if the quotation is a long one or an important statement by an important person.

> The Queen in her address to Parliament said:

3. In business letters after Dear Sir, Gentlemen, etc. (Here, too, you can see that the colon is saying: "I am writing the following.")

4. To set off the subtitle of a book.

> *All About Words: An Adult Approach to Vocabulary*

## Fine Points

Sometimes when both halves are complete sentences a semicolon or a colon or even a period may be used, depending on whether you want the second sentence to be an explanation of or supplement to the first or just another sentence containing a related thought.

> Senator Fulbright added: "I believe that the citizen who criticizes his country is paying an implied tribute: At the very least it means that he has not given up on his country, that he still has hopes for it."

(A semicolon or a period would do, though the colon shows that the second half is supplemental or explanatory. The colon is the more sophisticated mark of punctuation.)

Though a dash should not be used after a colon, it can sometimes substitute dramatically for it. But be wary.

This dismal book can be *summarized in one word—rubbish.* (The original sentence had a colon. The dash is a bit more dramatic.)

## REVIEW EXERCISE

Some of the following sentences call for semicolons or colons; some need other punctuation marks. Put in *all* the necessary marks. But be careful. Some sentences may require only a comma or even nothing. *No dashes, please.* The first ten sentences in the exercise are fairly easy to punctuate. You may find that the final ten require more thought.

1. Mr. Fleming is a graduate of three celebrated English educational institutions Eton Sandhurst and Fleet Street.

2. The other members of the delegation are Charles D. Cook Francis Carpenter and William Bradford.

3. Such a pitcher hurling toward such a batter poses a problem in ballistics what happens when an almost unhittable pitch is aimed at an almost superhuman batter.

4. Every fresh study reaches the same grim conclusion the world is on a treadmill when it comes to feeding the growing populations of developing countries.

5. The other stops will be Asunción Paraguay June 12 Santiago de Chile June 13 La Paz Bolivia June 15 and Lima Peru June 16.

6. The revival of dramatic classics is to one critic deplorable it seems to him a sign of the anemia of the modern age.

7. The evidence is incontrovertible therefore I urge you to act.

8. Among the few home remedies of that era that have survived only one is still prominent aspirin.

9. We are enclosing the information requested however our backlog of mail orders is so great we cannot promise that there will be seats available.

10. Sandy Koufax is the finest pitcher of modern baseball indeed he may be the best baseball has ever had.

11. We mean a nation free of those things that afflict a mans body and restrict his mind crime ignorance poverty and disease.

12. The building inspectors found no major violations nevertheless they insisted on the installation of brighter electric lights in the hallways.

13. Among the guests were Erich Leinsdorf director of the Boston Symphony Howard Hanson of the Eastman School of Music in Rochester and Rudolf Serkin and André Watts pianists.

14. The humanities are the study of man his languages his literature his philosophies and his culture.

15. There are many experts supported by popular opinion who believe that our national prestige makes any effort worth the cost no matter how great but there are also those who believe we can spend the money to better advantage on earth than by shooting into space.

16. Let me not pretend to learning I do not have though I studied Greek in college most of it to my shame has gone with the wind.

17. The skeptics admit something must have been seen the question to be answered is what was it.

18. In most espionage efforts there are three elements the individual who has access to secret material the contact man who persuades him to steal it and the agent who transmits it to where it is wanted.

19. Television is in the middle of a new controversy over old problems how good are its programs and who should make them better.

20. Think of all that has happened in the last five decades spaceships and penicillin computers and electric dishwashers air conditioners and atomic power five-day workweeks and movies in the skies.

## SHORTCUT

## QUOTATION MARKS

Radio made the words *quote* and *unquote* so popular that some people, when they are writing, use these words in addition to quotation marks. Only the quotation marks should be used, of course, for in writing they are the shortcuts we use for the words *quote* and *unquote.*

Notice how the use of quotation marks and related punctuation affects the meaning in each of the following pairs of sentences.

1. In which sentence is someone rebuking his friend for thinking badly of himself?
   *a.* You're always saying I'm stupid.
   *b.* You're always saying, "I'm stupid."

2. In which is there a hint of hurt pride?
   *a.* "Why are you so surprised?" he asked me.
   *b.* Why are you so surprised he asked me?

3. In which sentence does the scientist imply that he is not frightened?
   *a.* What great scientist recently wrote an article beginning with the three-word sentence, "I am frightened?"
   *b.* What great scientist recently wrote an article beginning with the three-word sentence, "I am frightened"?

## Recording Conversation

1. All conversation (except in play form) is indicated by quotation marks, preferably with a separate paragraph for each change of speaker.

| *Either* | *Or* (in play form) |
|---|---|
| "I am here at last," he shouted. | He (shouting): I am here at last. |
| "I am so glad," she sighed. | She (sighing): I am so glad. |

2. When the speech is interrupted by *he said, she replied,* etc. additional quotation marks are needed, as in this pre-TV anecdote:

> "What man," Benjamin Franklin was once asked, "deserves most to be pitied?"
>
> "A lonesome man," he replied slowly, "on a rainy day who does not know how to read."

Or this more modern example from a speech made by Dr. Anna Freud, seventy-five-year-old daughter of Sigmund Freud, at a congress of psychoanalysts, held in Vienna, as reported in *The New York Times* of July 31, 1971.

> "My father said that the first man to use abusive words instead of his fists was the founder of civilization," Miss Freud said, "and I would like to propose that the first man to use weapons instead of his fists was the originator of war."

## More on Interrupted Quotations

1. Before *he said* or *he asked,* we may have a comma, a question mark, or an exclamation point, but not a period.

> "What you say," he said, "is absolutely true."
> "I'm going home," he said. "Where are you going?"
> "Where are you going?" he asked. "I'm going home."

> "What a foolish thing to do!" he said. "I'm going home."

2. After *he said* or *he asked*, we may have a comma, a semicolon, or a period, depending upon the nature of the interruption.

> "I'm going," he said, "and I mean right now."
> "I'm going home," he said; "I can't stand it any longer."
> "*I'm* going home," he said. "You do what *you* wish."

## For Direct Quotations

The chief use of quotation marks, therefore, is to show that the writer is recording the exact words that were either written or spoken. If, for example, we wish to ascribe the sentence *Victory has a hundred fathers and defeat is an orphan* to the person who originally said it, we have to use quotation marks. We might do it in any one of the following ways:

> "Victory has a hundred fathers and defeat is an orphan," John F. Kennedy once said.

or

> John F. Kennedy once said, "Victory has a hundred fathers and defeat is an orphan."

or

> "Victory has a hundred fathers," John F. Kennedy once said, "and defeat is an orphan."

Notice that in each instance concluding commas and periods are placed within the closing quotation marks. The rule in the United States is to *place commas and periods inside closing quotation marks.*

Here are three more examples, showing the placement of the comma and the period within the closing quotation marks:

1. With five shows now rehearsing on Broadway, the mood is, in the word of one producer, "euphoric."

2. When Puck said, "I'll put a girdle round about the earth in forty minutes," Shakespeare's audience knew well enough that this was fantasy like the rest of *A Midsummer Night's Dream.*

3. Dr. William Haddon, Jr., said there was overwhelming evidence to show that "about one-half of our fatal crashes are initiated at least in part by the prior use of alcohol."

The British have somewhat different rules. In sentences like the three just given they would place the period or comma outside the closing quotation marks. The British are really more logical than we are, since the period or comma is not part of a quoted word, phrase, or clause. When long sentences are quoted, however, the British generally tuck the period inside the closing quotation marks.

Though the occasion does not arise often, *always place a semicolon or colon after the closing punctuation marks* In the following sentence either a semicolon or a colon might be used:

> There was reason to doubt him when he said, "I'll pay you back tomorrow"; he never had made good on any of his debts.

There is no special reason for our practice in the United States of always placing periods, commas, semicolons, and colons in a specific place. The rules have just been devised for simplicity and uniformity. The writer doesn't have to make decisions; he simply follows the rules.

There is, however, some room for variation when question marks and exclamation points are used. They must be placed where they are most useful and where they make the most sense. Notice the position of the question marks and the exclamation points in the following sentences:

"Is it going to rain?" he asked.

He asked, "Is it going to rain?"

"I never want to see you again!" he screamed.

He screamed, "I never want to see you again!"

Simple? Yes. But let's look at this sentence:

Did he say, "I'll never go there again"

Where shall we place the question mark now? Easy. The quoted words do not ask the question; the question is contained in *Did he say*. Therefore we write:

Did he say, "I'll never go there again"?

The question mark comes at the very end of the sentence, outside the quotation marks. Notice that there is no period after *again*. The question mark at the end is all the punctuation needed.

Now let us look at a sentence that presents a slightly more complex problem:

What character in the play says, "What's going to happen to all of us"

Here both the introductory statement and the quoted words are questions. Where do we place the question mark? Most people agree that it is more important to identify the quoted words as the question. We, therefore, place the question mark inside the final quotation marks:

What character in the play says, "What's going to happen to all of us?"

We do not use two question marks: one inside and one outside the quotation marks. One is enough.

Generally we treat the exclamation point with quotation marks exactly as we do the question mark. *Exclamation marks, like question marks, are placed outside the closing quotation marks unless the quotation itself is an exclama-*

*tion.* Notice the position of the exclamation marks in the following sentences:

> What a comedown for him to have to say, "I don't know the answer"!
> He screamed, "I'll never forgive him!"

(Note that there is no period after *answer* in the first sentence.

## CAUTION

1. Be sure you use quotation marks only when the exact words of the speaker are quoted. There are no quotation marks in the following sentences. Why not?

> The press secretary said there would be no party. A birthday cake had been ordered, he said, but the President and his wife planned to dine alone.

In spite of the phrase *he said,* we use no quotation marks, because we are not quoting the press secretary's exact words. He actually said, "There will be no party. They have ordered a cake, but the President and his wife plan to dine alone."

2. A comma does not follow *he said* if the word *that* intervenes:

> The press secretary said that the President and his wife plan to dine alone.

The exact words of the secretary are quoted, but the word *that* makes the comma superfluous and wrong.

3. When a quotation appears within a quotation, single quotes are used:

> "What American patriot," asked Miss Finch, "once said, 'A house divided against itself cannot stand'?"

## Quotations of More Than One Paragraph

When a quotation has more than one paragraph, quotation marks are used at the beginning of each paragraph but are only placed at the end of a paragraph when the quotation is entirely finished. This practice is exemplified in the following excerpt from the sports page of *The New York Times:*

> "There's no cure and it isn't getting any better," he told friends. "I can't throw the curve the way I used to. And I can't try to learn any new pitches, because that would bring new motions and new strains into play, and only disable me faster.
>
> "And I'm no masochist. I don't enjoy pain. I'll stand it because it's necessary to accomplish a goal, but there will come a point when I won't take it any more. I don't want to be crippled. It hurts, and it's going to continue to hurt, and it won't improve."

The same holds true for stanzas of poetry when they are quoted as below.

Three hundred years ago Sir John Suckling gave what may be considered definitive advice to lovesick youth when he wrote:

> "Why so pale and wan, fond lover?
> Prithee, why so pale?
> Will, when looking well can't move her,
> Looking ill prevail?
> Prithee, why so pale?
>
> "Why so dull and mute, young sinner?
> Prithee, why so mute?
> Will, when speaking well can't win her,
> Saying nothing do't?
> Prithee, why so mute?
>
> "Quit, quit for shame! This will not move,
> This cannot take her.

If of herself she will not love,
Nothing can make her;
The devil take her!"

## Other Uses of Quotation Marks

1. Quotation marks are placed around the titles of songs, short stories, short poems, essays, articles. They are also used to indicate chapter titles or other subdivisions of books. (The titles of longer works—books, magazines, newspapers, movies, operas, and full-length plays—are often indicated by quotation marks but underlining is generally preferred. In printed material, underlined titles are set in italics.) Some examples of the use of quotation marks around titles follow:

> I've just finished reading Somerset Maugham's short story "The Letter."
>
> "Stopping by Woods on a Snowy Evening" is one of Frost's most popular poems.
>
> "Where Do We Go from Here?" in last month's *Harper's* led to a heated argument.

(Notice in this last sentence that *Harper's* the name of a magazine, is in italics, If you had been writing this title by hand or on the typewriter, you would have underlined it to show that it should be italicized.)

2. Words used in a special or unusual way are sometimes enclosed in quotation marks. For example:

> Some foreign words have become "naturalized"; they are so much a part of our everyday speech that there is no need to set them off in italics.

(Here the word *naturalized* is enclosed in quotation marks because it is a somewhat special use of the word; generally we speak of people, not of words, as being naturalized.)

3. Slang expressions, colloquialisms, newly coined words, and technical expressions that are apt to be strange to the reader are often put in quotation marks. However, this is a device that should not be overworked. Some examples of its use follow:

> I always thought he was a real "weirdo."
>
> The Post Office Department "hiked" its rates again yesterday.
>
> He thought the design of the interior was too "campy."

4. If a nickname is not apt to be familiar to the reader, you can enclose it in quotation marks. You would not, for example, need to put quotation marks around *Babe* in Babe Ruth's name, but you might use them in this sentence:

> Though his name was Charles, for some reason he was called "Gus."

5. Foreign words and words referred to as words are sometimes enclosed in quotation marks. The preferred practice, however, is to underline these expressions as an indication that they should appear in italics.

> With his bench depleted by injuries the skipper sent in an untried rookie *faute de mieux*, and luckily the youngster delivered.
>
> Whenever he utters the word *but*, you know you're going to be subjected to a lengthy explanation in which you'll have little or no interest.

(If you were writing these sentences by hand or on the typewriter, you would underline the words italicized above.)

## CAUTION

1. Don't use quotation marks around expressions that have been accepted as part of our language.

2. Don't use quotation marks around the titles of your compositions or reports—unless your title happens to be a quotation that isn't too well known. (I wouldn't, for example, put quotation marks around To Be or Not to Be if I were going to use it as a title.)

## EXERCISE I: FROM INDIRECT TO DIRECT QUOTATION

In the following sentences change the indirect quotations to direct quotations. Revise the punctuation as necessary.

Example: Our teacher said that we had to have a parent's permission to attend the play.

Change to: Our teacher said, "You have to have a parent's permission to attend the play."

1. One of the marines said he still couldn't believe that he would be leaving for home soon.

2. The crowd cheered when their leader said that he would never surrender.

3. President Nixon today told Congress that he was making an immediate consignment of two million tons of food to East Pakistan.

4. The congressman said that official wiretapping is so widespread that nobody in Washington could be sure his telephones are private.

5. The students had appealed to him, the college president said last night, and a hearing had been set for 9 A.M. Monday.

6. When Dr. Gibbons was asked whether the council was setting up a lobby in Washington, he replied that they were using citizen influence to affect legislation.

## EXERCISE II: QUOTATION MARKS AND OTHER PUNCTUATION

Add all of the necessary punctuation marks to the following sentences.

1. Common or international English avoids phrases that are used primarily by Americans—such as cut it out or wait up. It relies instead on such expressions as stop it or wait for me which are universally understood.

2. I believe there was a King Arthur said Sir Mortimer Wheeler and the chances are 6 to 4 that he lived at South Cadbury.

3. Its like Hamlet Paul Edward who plays the CIA agent said everybody gets it in the end.

4. Dont kiss the babies she advised you'll lose the vote of the mother who thinks you're spreading germs.

5. Too many college programs Senator Fulbright said allow their liberal arts students to drift through their education without exposure to the exact sciences and the classical disciplines.

6. Its fantastic said Commander Charles Conrad Jr the command pilot of Gemini 11 I've got India at the left window and Borneo under my nose.

7. W. Somerset Maughams story The Verger is in our literature anthology.

8. The dance floor was in constant use and the jukebox regularly blared out Nancy Sinatra's These Boots Were Made for Walkin.

9. I always thought he was chicken and this last incident proves it.

10. Dr. Albert Schweitzer scorned every form of luxury. Once traveling by train he bought a third-class ticket. Why do you travel third class he was asked because there is no fourth class he replied.

### EXERCISE III: ASSORTED PUNCTUATION MARKS

Punctuate the following AP dispatch, paying special attention to quotation marks and the surrounding commas and periods but also including any other punctuation needed.

KANSAS HONORS GIRL
WHO URGED LINCOLN
TO GROW WHISKERS

Delphos, Kans., Aug. 8 (AP)—Gov William H Avery dedicated a monument here today to Grace Bedell Billings who wrote a letter to Abraham Lincoln suggesting he grow a beard

Mrs Billings who died in 1936 at the age of 88 was a homesteader with her husband G N Billings in 1869 She was 11 years old and lived at Westfield N Y when she wrote to Lincoln during the Presidential election campaign of 1860

On Oct 15 1860 after seeing Lincolns shaven face on a campaign poster young Grace wrote to him as follows

I have got four brothers and part of them will vote for you anyway and if you will let your whiskers grow I will try to get the rest of them to vote for you You would look a great deal better for your face is so thin All the ladies like whiskers and they would tease their husbands to vote for you and then you would be president

Four days later Lincoln responded stating in a letter to Grace

As to whiskers having never worn any do you not think people would call it a piece of silly affectation if I were to begin it now

But on Feb 16 1861 after he was elected president Lincoln stopped at Westfield and called for Grace to come forward

In recalling the incident later Mrs Billings said

He climbed down and sat with me on the edge of the platform Grace he said look at my whiskers Ive been growing them for you Then he kissed me I never saw him again

Lincolns letter to Mrs Billings was purchased last March 22 for $20000 by David Wolper a Hollywood television producer and collector of rare documents

The monument was dedicated by Governor Avery as part of the Ottawa County centennial celebration.

## HYPHENS

1. To which question can the answer be: "In a seafood restaurant"?
   *a.* Where can you see a man eating shark?
   *b.* Where can you see a man-eating shark?

2. In which company would you rather be personnel manager?
   *a.* In normal times the company I work for employs a hundred odd men and women.
   *b.* In normal times the company I work for employs a hundred-odd men and women.

3. In which are the advantages due to environment?
   *a.* A big-city child has certain advantages.
   *b.* A big city child has certain advantages.

4. Which refers specifically to the Trojan horse?
   *a.* Beware the gift-bearing Greeks.
   *b.* Beware the gift bearing Greeks.

In one of its chief uses the hyphen tells the reader that two (or more) words not ordinarily joined—or merged—are to be taken in combination as a unit to modify the noun that follows. Probably the longest such unit modifier is one that Theodore M. Bernstein of *The New York Times* used in a review: "The authors adopt an I-can-laugh-at-it-now-but-it-was-no-laughing-matter-at-the-time attitude." In such a series you must be sure you use hyphens to join all of the words that modify the noun.

We see hundreds of such combined, or unit, modifiers every day. Notice how the hyphen in the following phrases prevents us from misreading the phrase—just as the hyphens in the paired sentences at the beginning of the chapter did.

> an extra-base hit (not an additional base hit but one good for extra bases)
> a fine-tooth comb (not a fine toothcomb, which would be a comb for your teeth, but a comb that has closely set teeth)

Here are some more examples. You might try to figure out some of the distinctions made by the hyphens.

> small-scale attacks
> all-night discussions
> around-the-clock police protection
> eight-year-old son
> hard-to-please audience

(Note that in all cases if the hyphenated words were to follow the noun you would use no hyphens: for example, an audience that was hard to please.)

However, as in most punctuation where meaning is

clear and readability is not helped by using additional punctuation, we do not ordinarily use the hyphen:

child welfare plan
civil service examination
flood control agency
high school student
special delivery mail

## Participial Modifiers

The hyphen appears frequently in combinations in which one element is a present participle (verb form with an *-ing* ending) or a past participle (verb form with an *-ed* or *-en* ending):

| | |
|---|---|
| good-looking teen-ager | free-wheeling style |
| drought-stricken area | best-dressed woman |
| law-abiding citizens | rosy-fingered dawn |
| much-needed rest | well-groomed young man |

But if the past participle is modified by an adverb ending in *ly* we do not use the hyphen:

neatly dressed student
eagerly awaited telephone call
carefully performed duty
highly praised achievements

## Nouns from Verb Phrases

Verb phrases composed of a verb and a preposition usually become solid, unhyphenated words when used as nouns. For example:

| | | |
|---|---|---|
| to let down | *becomes* | a letdown |
| to drop out | *becomes* | a dropout |
| to splash down | *becomes* | a splashdown |
| to take over | *becomes* | a takeover |
| to break through | *becomes* | a breakthrough |

Exceptions are recently created combinations or any words that might not be instantly recognizable. Would you immediately know what a *puton, tiein, sitin,* and *comeon* were? That's why we hyphenate such words: *a put-on, a tie-in, a sit-in, a come-on.*

## Compound Words

The tendency in compound words is to avoid hyphens and write them either as two words or as one solid word. If the first part of the compound is a *one*-syllable word, the result is usually written as *one* word:

| | | |
|---|---|---|
| housekeeper | textbook | bookkeeper |
| bedroom | footnote | taxpayer |
| tugboat | shoemaker | lighthouse |

If the first part consists of a word of more than one syllable, the result is two separate words:

| | |
|---|---|
| lighthouse keeper | history book |
| living room | gentleman friend |
| sailing boat | dining car |

However, I find *troublemaker* and *tailorshop* given as solid words in Webster III. Therefore, the best rule of all is: When in doubt, consult a dictionary.

When two prefixes are combined with the same noun to form separate, consecutive words, there is no hyphen between *and* and the second prefix:

pro- and anti-Communist demonstrations
pre- and post-World War II conditions

## Prefixes and Combining Forms

There are certain prefixes and combining forms that usually are separated by a hyphen from the word they are attached to, but there is not always general agreement about them. Here is a list of some prefixes that appear before words (and that are not ordinarily a part of those words) with some indication of when the hyphen is used.

*self:* almost always takes the hyphen, as in *self-conscious, self-defeating, self-satisfied, self-control.*

*half:* is hard to pin down. When followed by a past participle it is generally hyphenated, as in *half-fried, half-witted* (but *halfhearted*).. It is hyphenated in *half-moon, half-truth, half-mast, half-dollar,* but written as one word in *halfback* and as two words in *half brother* and *half shell.*

*ex:* is generally hyphenated when followed by a noun, as in *ex-serviceman, ex-champion.* For dignitaries the word *former* is preferred to *ex-*, as in *former President Johnson, former chairman of the committee.*

*co:* is usually hyphenated before nouns, as in *co-author, co-pilot, co-star,* but generally becomes part of a verb, as in *cooperate* and *coordinate.*

*anti:* Despite its strong meaning *anti* usually becomes part of the word except when an *i* follows, as in *anti-intellectual.*

*re:* is hyphenated chiefly to avoid misreading such words as *re-form* (to form again) and *re-cover* (to put a new cover on).

Some Latin and Greek combining forms like *crypto-* (hidden), *neo-* (new), *pseudo-* (false), *quasi-* (almost like) nearly always take the hyphen except when they appear in established words like *cryptogram, neophyte,* or *pseudonym.*

## Before and After Capitals

Almost any prefix or combining form when joined to a word beginning with a capital letter has a hyphen:

anti-Communist pre-Columbian

mid-Atlantic
neo-Nazi
pro-British
un-American

When a word is made up of an initial capital letter we use the hyphen:

H-bomb
X-ray
T-shirt
V-necked
L-shaped
U-turn

## Numbers

When compound numbers or fractions are written out, we use the hyphen:

Forty-second Street
twenty-one
one-tenth
three one-hundredths

When the compound contains a numerical first element, we use a hyphen:

6-hour day
10-minute delay
36-inch ruler
42-foot boat

### EXERCISE WITH HYPHENS

Put in all necessary hyphens.

1. The play it safe, pass the buck, don't stick your neck out policy is sapping the vitality and morality of our people.

2. A 66 year old tuxedo clad pianist sat down at the keyboard today in a West German cafe to begin a 44 day, trans atlantic piano marathon.

3. Mid and late Victorian melodramas were far more sophisticated than those of earlier days.

4. The Defense Department is speeding up development of a strap on jet flying device that could make Buck Rogers green with envy.

5. Earlier the satellite hopping astronauts had pulled away from their own Agena rocket, to which they had been attached for nearly 30 hours.

6. The President said today that our overall objective should be to continue to move toward balance of payments equilibrium.

## REVIEW EXERCISE

Insert the necessary punctuation marks in the following passages:

1. Ernest A Seeman director of the University of Alabama Press writes that Miss Emily Dickinson of Amherst Massachusetts is fast becoming one of the most in of the in poets of the 1960s some eighty years after her death.

2. In short while its true that in a hitters world happiness is a home run it is also true that home runs like happiness seldom result from conscious eager pursuit.

3. There are now four radios in the average American household in other words practically every individual in this country owns his radio set. Auto radios alone are now installed in more than 60,000,000 U.S. cars in the peak radio popularity year of 1946 there were 6,000,000 auto radios. Overall around 242,000,000 radios are now being operated in the United States a figure greater than the total population.

4. The book A Left Handed Manifesto is well documented by the author he declares that there are twenty million left handed Americans and he also names a list of famous lefties from Alexander the Great the Greek conqueror to two former Beatles Paul and Ringo.

5. Nicolas Horberry a sort of modern day Phileas Fogg was off this week on another leg of his around the world tour a hitchhiking trip across the United States. But unlike the hero of Jules Vernes novel *Around the World in 80 Days* the twenty year old Englishman has 524 days in which to make his world tour.

# Answers

CHAPTER 1 (pp. 1–7)

PAIRED SENTENCES A. (p. 2): 1. b 2. a 3. b 4. b 5. b 6. b 7. a 8. b 9. a 10. a 11. a 12. b 13. b 14. a 15. b 16. a 17. b 18. b 19. b 20. b

PAIRED SENTENCES B. (p. 4): 1. b 2. a 3. a 4. b 5. b 6. b 7. a 8. b 9. b 10. b 11. a 12. a 13. b 14. a 15. a

CHAPTER 2 (pp. 8–17)

SELF-QUIZ (p. 15): 1. a (adjective) b (noun) c (verb) 2. a (noun) b (adjective) c (adverb) 3. a (verb) b (adverb) c (noun) d (adjective) 4. a (adverb) b (adjective) c (noun) d (preposition) 5. a (verb) b (noun) c (adjective) 6. a (conjunction) b (preposition) 7. a (preposition) b (adverb) c (noun) 8. a (adjective) b (noun) c (verb) d (adverb) 9. a (verb) b (adjective) c (noun) d (adverb) 10. a (interjection) b (adjective) c (adverb)

WORD FORMATION (p. 16)

A. 1. comparison (n.), comparative or comparable (adj.), comparatively or comparably (adv.) 2. confidence (n.), confident (adj.), confidently (adv.) 3. destruction (n.), destructive (adj.), destructively (adv.) 4. description (n.), descriptive (adj.), descriptively (adv.) 5. deceit (n.), deceptive (adj.), deceptively (adv.) 6. defiance (n.), defiant (adj.), defiantly (adv.) 7. exclusion (n.), exclusive (adj.), exclusively (adv.) 8. analysis (n.), analytic or analytical (adj.), analytically (adv.) 9. resentment (n.), resentful (adj.), resentfully (adv.) 10. subversion (n.), subversive (adj.), subversively (adv.)

B. 1. accidental (adj.), ly (adv.) 2. beautify (v.), beautiful (adj.), ly (adv.) 3. democratic (adj.), ally (adv.), democratize (v.) 4. grammatical (adj.), ly (adv.) 5. miraculous (adj.), ly (adv.) 6. mischievous (adj.), ly (adv.) 7. ominous (adj.), ly (adv.) 8. chaotic (adj.), ally (adv.) 9. apologize (v.), apologetic (adj.), ally (adv.) 10. prophesy (v.), prophetic (adj.), ally (adv.)

C. 1. generosity (n.), generously (adv.) 2. efficiency (n.), efficiently (adv.) 3. formalize (v.), formality (n.), formally (adv.) 4. frivolity (n.), frivolously (adv.) 5. loneliness (n.) 6. sincerity (n.), sincerely (adv.) 7. similarity (n.), similarly (adv.) 8. humidity (n.), humidify (v.) 9. immunize (v.), immunity (n.) 10. immobilize (v.), immobility (n.)

D. 1. unanimously (adv.), unanimity (n.) 2. hypocritical (adj.), ly (adv.) 3. tragic (adj.), ally (adv.) 4. crucial (adj.), ly (adv.) 5. contention (n.), contentious (adj.), ly (adv.) 6. curiosity (n.), curiously (adv.) 7. injunction (n.) 8. jeopardize (v.) 9. portend (v.), portentous (adj.), ly (adv.) 10. remedial (adj.), ly (adv.) 11. ecstatic (adj.), ally (adv.) 12. ambiguity (n.), ambiguously (adv.) 13. piety (n.), piously (adv.) 14. jocose (adj.), ly (adv.) 15. miscellaneous (adj.), ly (adv.) 16. climactic (adj.), ally (adv.) 17. apathetic (adj.), ally (adv.) 18. spatial (adj.), ly (adv.) 19. circumstantial (adj.) 20. prodigious (adj.), ly (adv.)

## CHAPTER 3 (pp. 18–30)

PRETEST (p. 18): 1. is 2. was 3. There are 4. were 5. is 6. stays 7. has 8. were 9. is 10. is 11. have 12. were

EXERCISE A (p. 21): 1. was 2. have 3. creates 4. are 5. is 6. has 7. is 8. breed 9. was 10. was 11. are 12. lies 13. there are 14. are 15. threatens 16. was 17. were, are 18. is 19. are 20. are 21. is 22. is 23. doesn't 24. runs 25. is

NOW TRY THESE (p. 24): 1. were 2. is 3. are 4. were 5. was 6. were 7. was 8. are

TRY THESE (p. 25): 1. were 2. was 3. are

EXERCISE B (p. 26): 1. is 2. are 3. are 4. is 5. is

LOOK MA (p. 27): 1. have 2. have 3. have 4. think 5. use 6. are 7. deal 8. themselves

FOREIGN WORDS (p. 29): 1. -on 2. -on 3. -um 4. -im 5. -um 6. -um

## CHAPTER 4 (pp. 31–49)

PRETEST (p. 31): 1. whoever 2. who 3. whom 4. who 5. whoever 6. whoever 7. whoever 8. whom 9. who 10. whom

NOW TRY THESE (p. 34): 1. whom 2. who 3. who 4. whosoever 5. whoever 6. who 7. who 8. who 9. whom 10. who 11. who 12. whom 13. whoever 14. who 15. whom

PRETEST ON *I* OR *ME* (p. 36): C = correct; W = wrong
1. C 2. W 3. W 4. C 5. W 6. W 7. W 8. C 9. C 10. W

PLAYING IT BY EAR (p. 37): 1. me 2. me 3. we 4. I 5. me 6. him 7. them 8. me 9. we 10. me 11. him 12. us 13. me 14. me

A FEW TO PLAY AROUND WITH (p. 39): 1. I 2. she 3. I 4. he 5. I

REVERSE ENGLISH (p. 40): 1. she 2. I 3. I 4. he 5. she 6. he 7. we 8. me 9. me 10. I

POSSESSIVES: PAIRED SENTENCES (p. 42): 1. a 2. a 3. a 4. b

PRETEST (p. 43): 1. England's, agitators' 2. yesterday's, nation's 3. children's 4. candidates' 5. Dickens' or Dickens's 6. scientists' 7. men's, ladies', children's, today's 8. history's 9. next year's, this year's 10. planners', world's

APOSTROPHES FOR POSSESSIVES (p. 47): 1. morning's 2. its 3. students', parents', teachers', people's 4. Twain's, Dickens' or Dickens's 5. Ulysses' 6. ladies', today's 7. It's, boys', men's 8. people's, ours 9. boys', theirs 10. its
children's, visitors' (p. 48)

POSSESSION WITH GERUNDS (p. 49): 1. his 2. your 3. my 4. his 5. his 6. our 7. my

## CHAPTER 5 (pp. 50–63)

PAIRS (p. 50): 1. b 2. a 3. b 4. b

NOW TRY THESE (p. 52): 1. went 2. haven't got 3. have known 4. have already done 5. have been working 6. has been 7. has been 8. made 9. have had 10. lived

EXERCISE A (p. 53): 1. have been, celebrated, hold, held, has been 2. have never been, am, saw, has not stopped, enjoyed, have made

PAST OR PAST PERFECT (p. 55): 1. came, had left 2. moved, had known 3. had waited, came 4. had already decided, asked 5. had never failed 6. said, had served 7. explained, had rejected 8. said, had not wanted 9. have concluded, are, had received 10. denied, was, had been

PRINCIPAL PARTS (p. 59): 1. did 2. came 3. led 4. lay 5. lied 6. laid 7. saw 8. paid 9. rang 10. beat 11. brought 12. sought 13. chose 14. ran 15. won 16. grew 17. drank 18. fled 19. gave 20. slew

IN SENTENCES (p. 59): 1. drank 2. saw 3. did 4. came 5. risen 6. gone 7. run 8. lying, threw 9. taken 10. swum 11. beat 12. led

SUBJUNCTIVES (p. 61): 1. hadn't been 2. were 3. had known 4. correct 5. had said 6. was 7. had been 8. correct or would be 9. had walked 10. had known

## CHAPTER 6 (pp. 64–76)

PAIRED SENTENCES (p. 65): 1. a 2. b 3. b 4. b 5. a 6. a

PRETEST (p. 65): 1. indistinctly 2. simply, flashily 3. beautiful 4. differently 5. delicious 6. beautifully 7. carefully 8. gracefully 9. nearly 10. well, badly 11. well 12. badly

EXERCISE CHIEFLY ON GOOD AND WELL (p. 68): 1. well 2. differently 3. sweet 4. seriously 5. well 6. well 7. well, regularly 8. well 9. cautiously 10. confident 11. different 12. marvelously 13. strange 14. bad, though badly is acceptable 15. sweet

EXERCISE ON COMPARATIVES (p. 71): 1. omit *more* 2. omit *more* 3. omit *most* 4. omit *more* 5. omit *more* 6. omit *more*

EXERCISE ON FINE POINTS (p. 73): 1. fewer 2. almost 3. fewer 4. many 5. deep, almost 6. fewer 7. almost 8. fewer 9. almost 10. fewer

EXERCISE ON DUE TO (p. 76): 1. Because of or on account of 2. Because of 3. Because of

## CHAPTER 7 (pp. 77–82)

PAIRS (p. 77): 1. a 2. a 3. a 4. a 5. a 6. b 7. a

TEST ON MISPLACED MODIFIERS (p. 79): 1. End sentence with *after President Lincoln's assassination* 2. Begin with *Before you start* 3. *aged,* etc. after *meats* 4. Begin with *On the CBS,* etc. 5. Begin with *By telephone* 6. *in other people* after *seek* 7. Begin with *As they were leaving* 8. *which never,* etc. after *watch* 9. Begin with *In a red,* etc. 10. *best* after *likes*

PARTICIPLE PAIRS (p. 80): 1. b 2. a 3. a 4. a 5. a

TEST ON PARTICIPLES (p. 82): 1. *When caught, the suspect still,* etc. 2. *I found,* etc. after *World War II* 3. After *powder, the candidate is bought by the voters,* etc. 4. After *Russia, an American may find the everyday chores,* etc. 5. After *driving, the Traffic Department is offering reprints,* etc. 6. After *fade, St. Louis will, I think, furnish,* etc. 7. After *years, Beethoven is still,* etc. 8. After *plane, I was given,* etc. 9. After *darkness, I was dazzled,* etc. 10. After *lake, I saw a fish,* etc. (Important: In each of these sentences, the participial phrase can always be changed to a subordinate clause, thus necessitating no change in the rest of the sentence. For example:

1. When the suspect was caught, he . . .

7. Although Beethoven has been dead for more than 150 years, his music . . .

8. When I entered the plane, the stewardess . . .

10. As I walked along the lake, a fish . . .

## CHAPTER 8 (pp. 83–109)

PAIRS (p. 83): 1. b 2. a 3. a 4. a 5. b 6. b 7. a 8. b 9. a 10. b 11. b 12. a 13. a 14. b 15. b 16. a 17. a 18. b 19. b 20. b

LIE VS. LAY (p. 98): 1. lying 2. lay 3. lie 4. lie 5. lying 6. lie 7. laid 8. had lain 9. lay 10. lay 11. lying

LIKE VS. AS (p. 101): 1. as 2. like 3. as if 4. the way (or as) 5. like 6. as if 7. as much, the way 8. like us 9. as if, as though 10. as if 11. like 12. as if

WORDS CONFUSED (p. 106): 1. accept 2. borrowed 3. among, affect 4. uninterested 5. species 6. effected, affected 7. lying 8. take 9. fortunate 10. allusion 11. complementary 12. besides, implied 13. the toes 14. climactic 15. adapt 16. flouted 17. imply 18. let 19. militated 20. implying 21. flaunt 22. effect 23. forcible 24. enormousness 25. self-depreciation 26. flout 27. infer 28. mitigate 29. venal 30. deduce, principle

## CHAPTER 9 (pp. 110–35)

SUPERFLUOUS WORDS (p. 119): Omit the following words in each case: 1. together 2. and 3. of 4. false 5. general and of opinion 6. with each other 7. more 8. as to 9. up 10. herewith 11. back 12. the fact 13. up 14. first 15. in the afternoon 16. and every 17. more 18. In my opinion or I think 19. on 20. only 21. of mine 22. more than 23. of the fact 24. In the 25. as to 26. back 27. or not 28. by all the members 29. as to 30. 's life

IDIOMS (p. 124): 1. Omit *about* 2. *Since it was raining we stayed at home* 3. Omit *about* 4. Change *with* to *to* 5. Change *to* to *by* or *at* 6. Change *with* to *of* 7. Preferably use *with* instead of *to* 8. Change *than* to *as* 9. Omit *of* 10. Insert *from* after *graduated* 11. Omit *of* 12. Change *from* to *of* 13. Change *on* to *in* 14. Change *in regards to* to either *in regard to* or *as regards* 15. Insert *on* or *upon* after *operated* or change to *undergo surgery*

DOUBLE NEGATIVES (p. 126): Omit or change the following words in each case: 1. hardly 2. Omit *hardly* or change *without* to *with* 3. n't 4. *n't* or use *either* and *or* 5. n't 6. *nowhere* to *anywhere* 7. *no* to *any* 8. *not* or change *unless* to *if* 9. not 10. *limit* to *increase*

PARALLEL STRUCTURE (p. 128): 1. (of) remaining 2. delightful 3. and placed 4. first, they lack a philosophy 5. and explain 6. and what your academic and professional goals are 7. and to take care of 8. what changes are necessary

MALCLICHÉS (p. 132): 1. log 2. omit *a* 3. thud 4. two peas in a pod 5. core 6. childhood 7. cut and dried 8. shop 9. to err is human 10. you could cut it with a knife 11. either like a horse or like a Trojan 12. terra firma 13. leech 14. at both ends 15. nutshell

## CHAPTER 10 (pp. 136–67)

PAIRS (p. 139): 1. b 2. b 3. b 4. a 5. a 6. b 7. b 8. b 9. a 10. b

THE MATHEMATICAL APPROACH (p. 142): 1. ss 2. ss 3. s 4. ss 5. s 6. s 7. ss 8. s 9. s 10. s 11. ss 12. s 13. ss 14. s 15. s 16. ss 17. s 18. ss 19. ss 20. s

WHICH VOWEL (p. 146): 1. e 2. a 3. a 4. e 5. o 6. o 7. o 8. e 9. e 10. a 11. o 12. o 13. i 14. a 15. a 16. a 17. a 18. a 19. e 20. o 21. a 22. a 23. a 24. a 25. a 26. o 27. o 28. a 29. o 30. e 31. i 32. a 33. a 34. i 35. a 36. e 37. e 38. i 39. a 40. e 41. o 42. a 43. a 44. o 45. e

46. i 47. a 48. y 49. i 50. a 51. i 52. o 53. a 54. a 55. e 56. a 57. o 58. a 59. a 60. o

DOUBLING CONSONANT (p. 154):
A. 1. yes 2. yes 3. no 4. yes 5. yes 6. no 7. yes 8. no 9. yes 10. yes 11. yes 12. yes 13. yes 14. no 15. no
B. 1. yes 2. yes 3. no, but sometimes spelled with two l's 4. yes 5. no 6. no 7. yes 8. yes 9. yes 10. yes 11. no 12. yes 13. no 14. yes 15. no

EI or IE (p. 154): 1. ie 2. ie 3. ie 4. ie 5. ei 6. ei 7. ei 8. ie 9. ei 10. ei

REWRITE (p. 154): 1. There . . . they're . . . their 2. It's . . . too . . . to . . . its 3. you're . . . your 4. whether . . . weather 5. have . . . 've . . . of 6. There . . . they're . . . their; there're . . . there'll 7. principal . . . principal . . . principle 8. then . . . than 9. loose . . . lose 10. desert . . . desert . . . dessert 11. who's . . . whose

SPELLING DEMONS (p. 155): 1. all right 2. accidentally 3. suspense 4. business 5. accommodate 6. conscious 7. sacrifice 8. resistance 9. coming 10. recommend 11. disappoint 12. grammar 13. mathematics 14. privilege 15. possesses 16. separate 17. sincerely 18. surprise 19. achievement 20. across 21. believe 22. beginning 23. valleys 24. author 25. repetition 26. tragedy 27. pursuing 28. writing 29. dissected 30. courageous 31. character 32. environment 33. description 34. serviceable 35. existence 36. humorous 37. imitate 38. immediately 39. definitely 40. necessary 41. prejudice 42. occasionally 43. occurrence 44. loneliness 45. casualties 46. stomach 47. murmur 48. consensus 49. villain 50. desiccated

SPELLING BONERS (p. 157): 1. cutlass 2. preyed 3. planned 4. sleigh 5. surely 6. infinitesimal 7. self-centered 8. congenital 9. dissertation 10. married 11. wielded 12. unanimously 13. gorged 14. single 15. masquerade

CAPITAL LETTERS (p. 160): President, Senate, Indians, Republicans, Democrats, Captain, Seventy-second Street, Norwegian, G.O., English, Michigan State University, Phi Beta Kappa, World War II, Ph. D., "An Inquiry into the Customs and History of the American Indian," Secretary of the Interior, Congressional Committees.

CHAPTER 11 (pp. 168–241)

INSTANT CLARITY (p. 169): 1. shoot, the attendant 2. after, Philip 3. saw, Danny Kaye 4. eating, the dog 5. past, ten years 6. before, World War I 7. cellar, steps 8. quickly, for 9. Lincoln, and 10. family, life

PERIOD PAIRS (p. 172): 1. b 2. a 3. a

SENTENCES (p. 173): 1. C 2. F 3. C 4. F 5. C 6. F 7. RO 8. RO 9. F 10. RO

SIGN (p. 175): PRIVATE? NO! SWIMMING ALLOWED

CLIVE (p. 176): When General Clive was a young man, he went to work as a clerk in India for the East India Company. One evening he was honored by an invitation to play cards with a party of young army officers of the Queen. A young captain whose name has never been told sat next to Clive. As he passed the cards to Clive, the captain said, "Cut." [*or* "Cut!"]

Clive rose and said quietly, "Have you discovered a new way to cut cards? You kept back a card when you handed them to me. You cheated!"

The other officers immediately jumped to their feet, amazed that one of their number had been accused of cheating. To settle the difficulty at once and to uphold the honor of the army, a duel was arranged with pistols at ten paces. As a nervous Clive and the confident captain stood facing each other, Clive's pistol accidentally exploded missing the captain's head only by inches.

It was now the captain's privilege—according to the laws of dueling—to shoot at Clive from where he pleased. He strode over to the young man deliberately and held the pistol to Clive's temple exclaiming, "What was that you said to me?"

"Captain," replied Clive slowly and steadily, "before you gave me those cards you took one out of the pack. You know you did. You cheated!" [*or* ."] The captain lowered his hand and then raised it again as if to fire. Again his hand dropped and he finally shouted, "You have the devil and God on your side, and I can't fight the three of you. I did cheat." [*or* !"]

Then he rushed out of the room. For a moment the officers remained speechless, being too stunned to do or say anything. Then recovering from their shock, one of them shouted, "Get after him. He's disgraced the uniform. He must be punished!" [*or* ."]

"Just a moment," Clive said blocking their way, "you didn't

think him a cheat a minute ago, did you? Yet he was just as much a cheat then. You were willing to see me murdered. Did you try to find out whether my accusation was just? No! That man treated me more fairly than you have."

Clive looked about the room, and when he had made a mental note of those present, he concluded, "If any of you in this room ever breathes a word against the captain, I promise not to be as charitable to you as he was to me."

RECOGNIZING ABBREVIATIONS (p. 179): 1. number, north 2. cubic centimeters 3. Honorable 4. Conscientious Objector 5. Senior 6. Registered Nurse or Royal Navy 7. versus (against) 8. postscript or public school 9. Junior 10. Doctor of Philosophy 11. Master of Arts 12. ante meridiem (before noon) 13. post meridiem (after noon) 14. Doctor of Medicine 15. Maryland 16. Parent-Teachers Association 17. Virginia 18. Veterans' Administration 19. Répondez s'il vous plaît (Please reply) 20. cash on delivery or collect on delivery 21. Rural Free Delivery

LATIN ABBREVIATIONS (p. 179): 1. *id est* (that is) 2. *circa* (about, around, approximately) 3. *confer* (compare or check) 4. *exempli gratia* (for example) 5. *et alii* (and others) 6. *et sequentia* (and the following) 7. *ibidem* (in the same place) 8. *opere citato* (in the work cited) 9. *quod vide* (which see) 10. *videlicet* (namely)

ADJECTIVES IN SERIES: PAIRS (p. 183): 1. b

USE OF COMMAS (p. 183): 1. clean, clear 2. none 3. none 4. none 5. screaming, high-pitched 6. full, rich

PAIRS (p. 185): 1. a 2. a 3. b 4. b 5. b 6. b 7. a 8. a

CLARITY (p. 186): 1. writing, such 2. watched, my father 3. way, things 4. leave, my parents 5. fired, the bullet 6. understand, the proposal 7. to, go 8. survive, thanks 9. alienated, better 10. been, given

COMPOUND SENTENCE (p. 192): 1. grass, and 2. San Francisco, and 3. home, and 4. them, and 5. afternoon, and 6. Brooks Robinson, and 7. mother, and 8. forces, and

BEFORE CONJUNCTIONS (p. 194): 1. wrong 2. optional 3. optional 4. wrong 5. wrong 6. wrong 7. wrong 8. wrong 9. optional 10. necessary for immediate clarity

DETOUR PAIRS (p. 199): 1. b 2. a 3. b 4. a 5. b 6. a 7. a 8. b 9. a 10. a

RELATIVE CLAUSES (p. 204): 1., who . . . death, 2. none 3. none 4. none 5., who . . . today, 6. none 7., who . . . San Francisco, 8., when 9., which . . . bomb, 10., which . . . art,

DOUBLE OR NOTHING (p. 207): 1., one . . . purpose, 2., once . . . dish, 3., one . . . caught, 4. none 5., a . . . diplomats, 6., the . . . planets, 7., a . . . Anderson, 8., court . . . Table, 9. none 10., eighteenth . . . contemporaries,

COMMAS FOR CLARITY (p. 208): 1., he 2. critics, 3., though 4. insignificant, 5. disease, 6. take out comma before *to* and place one before *headed* 7. Take out comma after *versed* and place one after *thoroughly* 8. defense, 9., while 10., despite

DETOUR MARKS (p. 211): 1. dashes 2. commas 3. dashes 4. brackets 5. commas 6. dashes 7. dashes or parentheses 8. dashes 9. dashes 10. commas 11. dashes 12. commas

REVIEW EXERCISE (p. 221): 1. Eton, Sandhurst, and Fleet Street 2. Cook, Francis Carpenter, and William Bradford 3. either ballistics: What . . . ? (sophisticated), or two sentences *ballistics. What . . . ?* 4. conclusion: The, or two sentences 5. Asuncion, Paraguay, June 12; Santiago de Chile, June 13; and so on 6. colon, semicolon, or period after *deplorable* 7. incontrovertible; therefore 8. prominent: 9. requested; however, 10. baseball; indeed 11. man's . . . mind: crime, ignorance, poverty, and disease. 12. violations; nevertheless, 13. Leinsdorf, director . . . Symphony; Howard Hanson . . . Rochester; and Rudolf Serkin . . . Watts, pianists. 14. man, his languages, his literature, his philosophies, and his culture. 15. experts, supported . . . opinion, . . . cost, no matter how great; but . . . space. 16. have; though . . . college, most . . . 17. seen; or. 18. elements: the individual . . . material, the contact . . . it, and . . . 19. problems: how good . . . 20. decades: spaceships and penicillin, computers . . . dishwashers, air conditioners . . . power; five-day . . .

QUOTATION MARKS (p. 223): 1. b 2. b 3. a

EXERCISE I (p. 232): 1. said, "I . . . that I . . ." 2. said, "I will never surrender." 3. told Congress: "I am making . . . Pakistan." 4. said, (or :) "Official . . . can be sure . . . private." 5. "The students have appealed to me," the college president said last night, "and a hearing has been set . . . Monday." 6. was asked, "Is the council . . . Washington," he replied, "We are using . . . legislation."

EXERCISE II (p. 233): 1. "Cut it out," "Wait up," . . . "Stop it,"

"Wait for me," 2. "I . . . Arthur," said . . . Wheeler, "and . . ." 3. "It's like *Hamlet* (or 'Hamlet')," Paul . . . said. "Everybody . . . end." 4. "Don't . . . babies," she advised. "You'll . . . germs." 5. "Too . . . programs," Senator Fulbright said, "allow . . . disciplines." 6. "It's fantastic," said Commander . . . Conrad, (or no ,) Jr., the command . . . Gemini 11. "I've . . . nose." 7. Maugham's . . . "The Verger" . . . 8. Sinatra's "These . . . Walkin'." 9. "chicken" 10. "Why . . . class?" he was asked. "Because . . . class," he replied.

EXERCISE III: Assorted Punctuation Marks (p. 234):

KANSAS HONORS GIRL
WHO URGED LINCOLN
TO GROW WHISKERS

Delphos, Kans., Aug. 8 (AP)—Gov. William H. Avery dedicated a monument here today to Grace Bedell Billings, who wrote a letter to Abraham Lincoln suggesting he grow a beard.

Mrs. Billings, who died in 1936 at the age of 88, was a homesteader with her husband G. N. Billings in 1869. She was 11 years old and lived at Westfield, N.Y., when she wrote to Lincoln during the Presidential election campaign of 1860.

On Oct. 15, 1860, after seeing Lincoln's shaven face on a campaign poster, young Grace wrote to him as follows:

"I have got four brothers and part of them will vote for you anyway, and if you will let your whiskers grow I will try to get the rest of them to vote for you. You would look a great deal better, for your face is so thin. All the ladies like whiskers and they would tease their husbands to vote for you and then you would be President."

Four days later, Lincoln responded, stating in a letter to Grace:

"As to whiskers, having never worn any, do you not think people would call it a piece of silly affectation if I were to begin it now?"

But on Feb. 16, 1861, after he was elected President, Lincoln stopped at Westfield and called for Grace to come forward.

In recalling the incident later, Mrs. Billings said: (or ,)

"He climbed down and sat with me on the edge of the platform. 'Grace,' he said, 'look at my whiskers. I've been growing them for you.' Then he kissed me. I never saw him again."

Lincoln's letter to Mrs. Billings was purchased last March 22 for $20,000 by David Wolper, a Hollywood television producer and collector of rare documents.

The monument was dedicated by Governor Avery as part of the Ottawa County centennial celebration.

PAIRS (p. 235): 1. a 2. b 3. a 4. b

EXERCISE WITH HYPHENS (p. 240): 1. play-it-safe, pass-the-buck, don't-stick-your-neck-out policy. 2. 66-year-old tuxedo-clad . . . 44-day, trans-Atlantic 3. Mid- and Late-Victorian 4. strap-on 5. satellite-hopping 6. over-all . . . balance-of-payments.

REVIEW EXERCISE (p. 241):

1. Ernest A. Seemann, director of the University of Alabama Press, writes: "Miss Emily Dickinson of Amherst, Massachusetts, is fast becoming one of the most 'in' of the 'in' poets of the 1960's (or 1960s)—some eighty years after her death."

2. In short, while it's true that in a hitter's world happiness is a home run, it is also true that home runs like happiness seldom result from conscious, eager pursuit.

3. There are now four radios in the average American household; in other words, practically every individual in this country owns his own radio set. Auto radios alone are now installed in more than 60,000,000 U.S. cars; in the peak radio popularity year of 1946, there were 6,000,000 auto radios. Overall, around 242,000,000 radios are now being operated in the United States—a figure greater than the total population.

4. The book *A Left-Handed Manifesto* (or quotation marks) is well-documented by the author. He declares that there are twenty million left-handed Americans, and he also names a list of famous lefties, from Alexander the Great—the Greek conqueror—to two former Beatles, Paul and Ringo.

5. Nicolas Horberry, a sort of modern-day Phileas Fogg, was off this week on another leg of his around-the-world tour—a hitchhiking trip across the United States. But unlike the hero of Jules Verne's novel *Around the World in 80 Days* (or quotation marks), the twenty-year-old Englishman has 524 days in which to make his world tour.

# Index